AN AMERICAN CONVERSION

ONE MAN'S DISCOVERY OF BEAUTY AND TRUTH IN TIMES OF CRISIS

DEAL W. HUDSON

A Crossroad Book
The Crossroad Publishing Company
New York

The Crossroad Publishing Company
481 Eighth Avenue, New York, NY 10001

This book is typeset in 12/17 Goudy Old Style.

Printed in the United States of America

Library of Congress Cataloging-in-Publication Data

Hudson, Deal Wyatt.
    An American conversion : one man's discovery of beauty and truth in times of crisis / Deal W. Hudson.
        p. cm.
    Includes bibliographical references and index.
    ISBN 0-8245-2126-9
    1. Hudson, Deal Wyatt. 2. Catholic converts – Biography.
I. Title.
    BX4668.H83A3 2003
    248.2'42'092 – dc22
                                      2003017235

1 2 3 4 5 6 7 8 9 10   08 07 06 05 04 03

To Hannah

What is deep as love is deep, I'll have
Deeply. What is good as love is good,
I'll have well. Then if time and space
Have any purpose, I shall belong to it.
If not, if all is a pretty fiction
To distract the cherubim and seraphim
Who so continually do cry, the least
I can do is to fill the curled shell of the world
With a human deep-sea sound, and hold it to
The ear of God, until he has appetite
To taste our salt sorrow on his lips.

—Christopher Fry, *The Lady's Not for Burning*

CONTENTS

One	Telling the Story	11
Two	No Time for Beauty	16
Three	Tangoing with Baptists	24
Four	Away from Fundamentalism	30
Five	The Relief of Objectivity	38
Six	Starting with Sophocles	46
Seven	Some Disconnects	53
Eight	Defending Woman	61
Nine	Teaching the Absolute	66
Ten	The Bird Sings	77

Contents

Eleven   My Nun Story   84

Twelve   A Letter from St. Louis   92

Thirteen   Learning to Dance   103

Fourteen   Not an Angel   111

Fifteen   Beauty and Conversion   122

Sixteen   Beauty Will Save the World   130

Seventeen   Catholic Novels   134

Eighteen   Contrasting Aesthetics   144

Nineteen   Julian Green   152

Twenty   Meeting Maritain   161

Twenty-One   Quick-Ey'd Love   174

Photo Credits   186

Index of Names   187

✛ One ✛

TELLING
THE STORY

NEARLY TWENTY YEARS AGO, at the age of thirty-four, I was confirmed in the Catholic Church. That day twenty years ago was, undoubtedly, a new beginning for me. By that time I had been a Southern Baptist for sixteen years, since as a philosophy student at the University of Texas I had walked the aisle to accept Jesus Christ "as my Lord and Savior." Nothing that has happened since then has caused me to regret that decision to be baptized. And it was, in God's providence, my first step toward becoming a Catholic.

Converts are often asked to tell their stories. There are good reasons for telling them as well as a few bad ones. I am telling mine now to challenge readers to recognize the necessity of ongoing conversions in their own lives.

I don't want my story to be used against the denomination that I converted from, or to leave the
impression that my life is filled with past glories but
no present ones. And most of all, I don't want the
reader to assume that the greatest interior drama of
the Christian life belongs to converts.

In fact, we are badly in need of a body of literature
about the "reverts" who have struggled heroically
through the confusion of the modern Church to find
firm footing on our sacred deposit. And it's easy to
overlook the cradle Catholics who began on the right
foot and loyally stuck it out through generations of
confusion and, now, scandal.

My first conversion was a conversion to the love
of Christ, pure and simple. I was a nineteen-year-
old junior at the University of Texas-Austin studying
philosophy. My world consisted of reading Plato in
the midst of a burgeoning hippy culture, an emerging fascination with drugs, and the excitement of a
victorious Texas Longhorn football team.

Like all teenagers entering adult life, I thirsted for
the bonds of genuine fellowship to compensate for
the kind of disappointment most of us experience
in family life. I found this fellowship in a Southern
Baptist church.

When I walked the aisle of the Ridglea West Baptist Church in Fort Worth, Texas, I did it not only for the promise of grace and forgiveness but also for the security of a spirit-filled community. Grace meant that I would be given the power to look beyond my own concerns and will the good of others; forgiveness meant that I could make a fresh start. The generosity I witnessed among these humble Christians of modest means testified that the Gospel they preached could truly be lived.

I believed this because all the years I spent in the community of Baptists I consistently met people who worked sacrificially for others. Their church services were nothing less than celebrations of the shared concern and good feeling that Baptist piety, at its best, engendered among them.

When I became president of the Baptist Student Union at the University of Texas-Austin, I began to confront aspects of evangelical culture that eventually caused me to look elsewhere in the Christian tradition for my spiritual home. The fact that I studied philosophy was itself, to some Baptists, a reason to doubt my sincerity about Christ. Baptists, I was told, are, after all, the "people of the Book." I was told that everything I would need to know about life, morality, theology, and even some science was to be found in the revealed Word. I was warned against becoming "puffed up" with the pride of human wisdom.

I took these warnings seriously, but something seemed wrong about a Christian outlook that excluded all the world's greatest writers and artists from the conversation about truth. Indeed, as I read the history of philosophy — especially Plato, Aristotle, Descartes, Hume, Kant — I discovered deep affinities in the Western intellectual tradition with the Christian worldview that I was learning through regular Scripture study. In other words, without knowing its importance in the Catholic tradition, I was seeking the harmony of the faith and reason taught by the Church.

I never disputed the fact that Scripture should receive pride of place in the hierarchy of wisdom, or that a thorough grounding in biblical interpretation should not be superseded in favor of the tradition of great books. But when I argued for the benefit of such a synthesis I was dismissed as someone who was playing with fire and was about to be burned.

I chose to attend Princeton Theological Seminary instead of a Southern Baptist seminary because the Princeton curriculum included courses in philosophy, the history of doctrine, and the arts. In fact, my visit to a local Southern Baptist seminary confirmed my intuition that the Baptist commitment to education was shackled by fear of anything that was not explicitly tied to the study of Scripture. This fear was often refracted through a pompous dismissal of the arts and philosophy, which I found unnecessary and disappointing.

But I remained loyal to the denomination that had nurtured me during my college years, and while attending seminary, I founded the Baptist Student Union at Princeton University and tried in vain to start a mission church in central New Jersey. I was licensed to preach and became active among Southern Baptists in the New York–New Jersey area. Several times the larger-than-life president of the seminary, Dr. James McCord, tried to talk me into taking the Presbyterian route, but, for the time being, I hung on to the evangelical fervor of my Texas Baptist background.

✛ Two ✛

NO TIME FOR BEAUTY

URING MY BAPTIST YEARS, I was always being encouraged to witness, to tell people, preferably strangers, about my faith in Jesus Christ and hope they would be saved as a result. I've always admired this trait among evangelicals and definitely prefer it to the snooty avoidance of discussing personal faith that you find mainly among the upper class. Catholics could learn *much* from the zeal of their evangelical counterparts.

But there were times when the insistence on witnessing was treated as giving "proof" of one's faith rather than simply testifying to it. In other words, if you didn't talk about it enough, it didn't really exist, or if you didn't offer to bring up the topic of Jesus in the most incongruous circumstances, you weren't really a committed Christian.

I found my dilemma symbolized by my reaction to the guy who kept getting his yellow "John 3:16" sign on camera at major sporting events. I always wondered why he thought that antagonizing viewers would lead them to faith in Christ.

I was always considered by my academic and artistic friends to be all-too-ready to talk about my faith. As far as I knew I never provoked eye-rolling, but I certainly got close. My staunch Baptist friends wondered why I would talk about anything other than Jesus.

Later, when I was a graduate student at Emory, I became the associate minister of youth and education at the venerable Druid Hills Baptist Church on Ponce de Leon Avenue in Atlanta. Once one of the leading churches in the Southern Baptist Convention, Druid Hills was now struggling to cope with the urban environment that was slowly surrounding it. The congregation consisted mostly of those white middle-class congregants still living in the neighborhood along with a slightly more affluent crowd who had moved farther out from the city.

My job was to run the youth group, consisting of grades seven through college, as well as the Sunday

School and summer Vacation Bible School. Every Wednesday night after the weekly dinner and prayer meeting, I would lead my entire brood in a Bible study. In addition, I started to introduce them to film, drama, and novels directly relevant to Christian education. This provoked some skepticism and mild protest from their parents. Why, they asked, would I expose my youth group to anything other than the Bible?

For example, I mounted the medieval mystery play *Herod* to be performed on Christmas Eve in the sanctuary of Druid Hills Baptist Church by members of my youth group. The performance, directed by a theater friend of mine, came off powerfully, reaching its peak when Herod shakes his fist at God and calls for the killing of all children in the kingdom under the age of three. The Herod play belongs to a cycle of religious dramas that were performed regularly in the Middle and late Middle Ages in Catholic Europe. The Catholic imagination at that time had grown accustomed to seeing biblical stories embellished by theatrical, often funny and bawdy, treatment.

Alas, after all the weeks of work, those who attended the performance, with the exception of the proud parents, seemed shell-shocked. They told me that this had not been appropriate for Christmas Eve when we should be celebrating the birth of the Christ child. They weren't expecting the bloody babies strewn across the stage in the form of scarlet scarves pulled from the pockets of grieving mothers.

When asked why I had delivered such a disturbing message during the joyous season of Christmas, all I could say was that it was part of the Bible's Christmas narrative, even if nobody paid any attention to it. Evidently, among the "people of the Book" parts of the Bible were considered off limits. The problem was no one had let me in on the secret.

Witnessing as a Southern Baptist had a set of rules, which, though unwritten, exerted a strong conforming influence on believers. You witness by speech. You talk about your "personal relationship with Jesus Christ." Get away from the script, the precise rhetoric and diction, or decide to pass on an opportunity to witness and you risk your good standing, as I would one day find out. I had come to meet Jesus Christ through the love that Baptists shared with one another. We used to sing "They will know we are Christians by our love," but the strength of their fellowship had to be superseded by words, lots of words.

Frederick Delius – "Though an atheist and admirer of Friedrich Nietzsche, Delius set spiritual longing to music like no one else I had ever heard."

My first breaking point came quite by accident several years later while on a trip from Princeton Theological Seminary to Pittsburgh. I went there to visit a good friend, ten years older than myself, an accomplished physicist, who had been a member of the Fort Worth congregation that had witnessed my conversion. The other reason for visiting Pittsburgh was to visit another friend, whom I had never met but with whom I had been corresponding for several years about classical music, especially the music of the English composer Frederick Delius.

The music of Delius had become very important to me at seminary. I had stumbled across Ken Russell's film *The Song of Summer* late one night on PBS and found myself mesmerized by the music of this composer, who the conductor Sir Thomas Beecham had called "the last great apostle in our time of romance, emotion, and beauty in music." Though an atheist and admirer of Friedrich Nietzsche, Delius set spiritual longing to music like no one else I had ever heard. His setting of Whitman verses in *Sea Drift* remains for me a touchstone of spirituality in music.

My musical friend in Pittsburgh had been very generous to me through the mail, sending me books and records, as well as his lengthy letters. He had written to me out of the blue, having heard of my interest in Delius from a member of the Delius Society in England. When I told my Baptist friend that I planned a visit with my musical pen pal, his face turned very serious, and he said: "You plan on telling him about Jesus, don't you?" Frankly, I hadn't thought about it, though I didn't say that. I felt guilty and angry.

I went to see my musical friend and enjoyed a wonderful evening discussing all kinds of illicit things, from Nietzsche to twelve-tone music; we even drank some wine. On the way back to the Baptist physicist's house, where I was staying, I asked myself if I was going to lie to him. I knew he would ask if I had "witnessed." At the breakfast table I told the truth. Once again I was informed of my probable eternal resting place, and of my musical friend's as well. In the car on the way back to Princeton I wept.

To this day I can still see in memory those miles of road on the Pennsylvania Turnpike where I realized I was fundamentally different from those good people who had helped me so much in finding my faith.

People talk about religion making them feel guilty about drinking, dancing, sex, and so forth. But at that moment I felt guilty about my mind, my hunger for learning, and about my love of music. This is the most serious and paralyzing guilt of all, because it is guilt about being human, guilt about being the kind of creature God made you, guilt about exercising the potencies that God himself placed within you — guilt about life itself. By the time I reached Princeton, I had begun to suspect, however dimly, that I was no longer a Baptist, that I had been cut free. It would take many years and many other experiences before I knew where I should go.

✠ *Three* ✠

TANGOING WITH BAPTISTS

T HERE WERE SEVERAL OTHER defining moments during my three years at Princeton that made me question being a Southern Baptist. The summer before my senior year I received an invitation to lead a seminar on theology in film for Southern Baptist college students at a retreat center in Ridgecrest, North Carolina. I chose four films that I considered the most pertinent to theological treatment at that time: *Last Tango in Paris*, *A Clockwork Orange*, *Jesus Christ Superstar*, and *Fiddler on the Roof*. With four of my Baptist Princeton University students, I drove down to North Carolina, the heart of Billy Graham country.

Keep in mind, I did not show the films. I merely announced that I was going to discuss them. I expected a group of fifty students, but when I walked in the room there were hundreds. In the front row sat eight scowling young men with Bibles open on their laps. It was clear they were not there to enjoy the discussion, but rather to put me in my place for daring to speak openly about movies that contained sexually explicit scenes.

Some of my Princeton students who had come along took me aside before the first lecture and told me not to worry; if things got rough they were going to act as my bodyguards. The discussion was lively. No punches were thrown, but I was told in clear terms that I had introduced a Satanic influence into a spiritual retreat.

The next day, the national president of Baptist Student Ministries told me that a group of students were fasting and praying that my influence would not corrupt the students in my seminar. He asked if there were other movies I could discuss. I told him that since I was merely talking about the movies and not showing them, I didn't understand the outrage. He explained to me that the core of the problem was that I had seen the movies. How could I have made myself vulnerable to these dangerous images? I told him that thus far I had avoided imitating Marlon

Brando and Malcolm McDowell and that it was a safe bet I would not imitate them in the future.

That night an even larger group greeted me. This time one of my Bible-wielding critics brought his young son in the hope that his presence would keep me from discussing *A Clockwork Orange.* I wasn't deterred. The session nearly became physical, and several of my students came forward and stood beside me during the question and answer session. But they weren't nearly as large as the Bible-toters in the front row. As the seminar ended, it occurred to me that whatever career I might have looked forward to among Southern Baptists was in serious jeopardy.

The next semester I signed up for a reading course on the theology of St. Augustine with Dr. Karlfried Froelich, one of the finest teachers of anything I have ever encountered. Froelich was a devout Lutheran who embodied the greatness of theological study from the heart of Europe. The only requirement he gave me for the course was to read as many of Augustine's books as I could. He explained that most people read only *The Confessions* and never encountered the richness of Augustine's other treatises, or his letters, sermons, commentaries, and writings against heretics. He added, "Don't worry about trying to read all of Augustine. No one has ever done that."

I started with *On the Trinity*. It was one of those reading experiences that change your life. It was akin to what I saw in my first reading of Plato's *Apology*: a totally original mind whose grasp of ideas and command of argument is cumulatively overwhelming. What particularly impressed me was that a theologian could integrate history with biblical interpretation, philosophy, rhetoric, psychology, and experience. Augustine brings all these tools to bear, creating a vast range of analogies seeking to understand the Trinity as the love shared among the Father, the Son, and the Holy Spirit. Beginning with Scripture, Augustine moves from the sense world to human contemplation and the divine life, finding images of the Trinity at every level. He continually returns to psychological analogies that find the image of the Trinity reflected in the dynamics of human nature, particularly the powers of the mind to remember, to understand, and to love.

Now I realized the power and possibility of theology. I wondered why nothing I had encountered in

St. Augustine – "What particularly impressed me was that a theologian could integrate history with biblical interpretation, philosophy, rhetoric, psychology, and experience."

the Baptist tradition had this kind of vast comprehension of humane learning and culture. I came to see that when you reject tradition, culture, the arts, and works of reason, theology becomes little more than elaborate footnotes to biblical criticism. Baptist scholars, predictably, are marvelous interpreters of Scripture and great homilists.

Augustine's capacity for synthesis was based upon his grounding in the metaphysical tradition of classical Greece and Rome. In other words, Augustine possessed an intellectual framework that enabled him to mediate different sciences and truth claims into a coherent Christian perspective. In short, I found in Augustine an example of the synthesis of faith and reason that I had struggled to defend while an undergraduate at the University of Texas.

I knew nothing about the Catholic Church at that time in my life. If someone had given me a test on the nature of the Catholic Church — its priesthood, its sacraments, or its history — I would have flunked. I had never even met a Catholic priest. That would soon change.

✦ *Four* ✦

AWAY FROM FUNDAMENTALISM

I WANT TO TAKE CARE when speaking of the old friends who helped me to find my way. I owe these friends my constant thanks. Yet gratitude does not require me to be silent about the joys of the road that came farther ahead and my reasons for walking it. The ecumenist may judge this confession harshly, but I offer it in hopes of helping someone, like myself, who finds himself torn between the fellowship that nurtured him and the fellowship in which he knows he can flourish.

The year 1971 was the winding down period of the Vietnam War, and Watergate was just around the corner. It was a difficult time and the temptation was to be pushed toward extremes. Whether I was with my Baptist Student Union students or with the congregation of my mission church in Montville, New Jersey, I continually felt that all of them wanted a kind of truth that I could not give them — because God did not offer it. In fact, God had revealed something more, a Word that continued to be spoken through the Body of Christ. They wanted a revelation without a history, an inspired Bible undefiled by human hands, moral principles needing no interpretation, and worst of all, they wanted me to become a ministerial know-it-all and an evangelical bully.

I couldn't do it, even though I could see in their eyes how much they wanted it, and how much I could profit by it.

What seemed plain common sense to me then, as it does now — that God wants us to use our minds to understand and to glorify him — did not appear so obvious to many of my charges, or to their pastors. I can still remember the shock I felt when I was taken to lunch by the president of the Campus Crusade for Christ at the University of Texas and told that if I continued to study philosophy I would likely go to hell. I think it was prophetic that I didn't, even for a moment, feel any threat of damnation as a result of his remark. Instead, I wondered what he feared, and what was lacking in his understanding of faith that made it necessary to live without knowledge of history and ideas.

Truth must belong to God, no matter who utters it or how it is found. If so, why should we be afraid of it?

Thus, in the very first months of my Christian faith, I met head on one of many narrow prejudices, justified in the name of Jesus Christ and in the cause of salvation, that I was to grapple with for the next sixteen years. You might wonder what kept me so long in their fellowship. Obviously, not all Baptists thought I was going to hell; I received encouragement from many people who hoped that together we could change the direction of the denomination. I held out the same hope.

Historians of religion like Martin Marty remind us to distinguish between charismatics and fundamentalists. Although the two groups may use some of the same language and avow the same doctrinal formulae, the differences between the two are significant, as their occasional rifts demonstrate. Some charismatics, though, are more dangerous then fundamentalists. Those are the ones who eschew any common credo, except for their inspired feelings. In contrast, fundamentalists have a fairly well defined party line and must bow to an accepted standard of inerrant interpretation, which makes their leaders less disposed toward a self-indulgent theology, though they may indulge in other things.

Charismatics, on the other hand, who listen only to themselves and their inspired leaders, consider anyone who isn't "in the spirit" to be "of the flesh." (St. Francis was inspired, but obedient.) Fundamentalists, at least, have a standard, even if misshapen. And we always need to remember that Catholicism spawns its own twisted versions of the charismatic and the fundamentalist.

There were and still are so many good people among Southern Baptists who do not embrace the anti-intellectual attitudes of fundamentalists or their doctrines of biblical literalism. Though more and more mainline Baptists are adopting fundamentalist attitudes and credos, such is not their theological heritage. Fundamentalism in America is a recent phenomenon, although we could put it on a family tree of religious attitudes going as far back perhaps as Pythagoras.

I never really tried to be a fundamentalist, although I tried very hard to be a Baptist. Fundamentalism looked to me to be proud at the core: it promised a kind of truth that it could not deliver and depended upon the coercive force of close-knit social groups to enforce obedience.

Fundamentalism has been successful because it has been able to take advantage of hurt and lost people in a confusing age. Its tactics rely not only upon our need to belong to a community, which fundamentalists offer at the price of the full Gospel, but also upon the popular identification of truth with the ideal of science. This fundamentalist ideal "scientific" truth has no actual counterpart in the practice of empirical and social science itself. It's an ideal of truth that operates in the same cloud of authority that once enveloped Darwin, Freud, and Einstein.

Fundamentalism was, in part, a response to these thinkers that ended up lowering the Christian faith to their level. Darwin, Freud, and their followers claimed to have proven scientifically false central tenets of revealed Christianity.

Fundamentalists made the mistake of trying to meet Darwinists and Freudians on their own ground by creating a pseudo-science of biblical interpretation based upon literalism and inerrancy. Given such a fragile starting point we can understand why fundamentalism fueled the anti-intellectual and anti-Catholic fires still burning in American culture.

I met anti-Catholicism in my very first Sunday School class after becoming a Baptist. I was told that Catholics, as idolators of Mary and Pope, were not really Christians and probably going to hell. I thought, at the time, that something must be wrong with such a dismissal of a Church stretching back so far in history. When I summoned the courage to raise that question, I was told that Baptists themselves had existed since the time of the New Testament but had not succumbed to idols. This attitude that Catholics needed saving soon became an action item, for me.

In the heat of a Texas summer, I boarded the church bus, with Ridglea West Baptist Church painted across the side, bound for San Benito, a dusty Texas town just north of the Mexican border. With the help of the youth group, our minister was going to hold a tent revival for the immigrant workers, all of whom were, of course, Catholic. The thought passed through the back of my mind that we weren't really converting these Catholic children to Christianity but just opening the door to a rival version. I squelched that thought in the midst of brethren who were convinced that the issue was nothing less that their eternal salvation.

Even though I had been a Baptist convert for less than a year, I was asked by our pastor to deliver a sermon at the revival meeting. As I looked around at the heat, dust, and poverty of the town, it was clear that our revival was the most exciting thing in town. Here we were, thirty or so attractive, well-presented Anglos singing songs about love and total acceptance to children who obviously had very little. Our services culminated with the powerful bass voice of our pastor, an extraordinarily good preacher and man, who made the call of salvation seem irresistible. Standing in the pulpit before all those bright faces of the Hispanic children, I felt a heavy weight fall on my shoulders: I didn't feel ready or prepared for the responsibility of trying to change these children's lives. Though I could mock the Bible-clutching and the imploring hands reaching toward the sky, I lacked the basso profundo, the dramatic gravitas, of our minister. At the end of my comments, as awkward as they must have been, a young boy, aged eleven or twelve, came forward to "accept Jesus Christ" as his "Lord and Savior." When he came forward during the singing of "Just As I Am," I didn't know what to say to him or what to do with him. Then the preacher came to the rescue.

During the next few days he followed me around like I was his new hero.

A few weeks later I returned to Austin for my senior year at the University of Texas. When my Aunt Lucile asked my what I had been doing that summer, I told her about the revival in San Benito. Her face turned dark with disapproval as she asked why I would try to convert Catholics to a faith they already hold. She was speaking aloud my own doubts, but I wasn't willing at the time to let the implications sink in.

✠ Five ✠

THE RELIEF OF OBJECTIVITY

ONE OF THE ATTRACTIONS of fundamentalism is the certainty proclaimed by its preachers and adherents. Fundamentalism paints a world in black and white so there is no doubt where the believer stands in relation to good versus evil or truth versus falsehood. But the certainty of faith does not require such over-promising. This is the certainty that arises when the truths of faith are allied with what the human intellect knows from observing God's creation.

The Catholic Church stands for a conception of reality very different from that preached by the fundamentalist version of Protestantism. Reality in the Catholic tradition is objective in a way that the recent generations have rejected, and desperately need to reclaim.

My father was raised as a natural Aristotelian, although he never read a word of philosophy. In fact, he strongly objected to my early choice of vocation as a teacher of philosophy. But he understood, as did those of his generation, that values belong to the world outside the mind, that the mind discovers them through the course of experience and reflection. The meaning of life is not something a person invents. It is "out there" and has to be wrested or received from the world as it is. Nature, in other words, precedes our choices and our understanding. Catholics of an older generation called this the natural law.

The last few generations have been raised as natural Nietzscheans, again without having read the so-called father of existentialism. Values are created by each individual. There is no single meaning to life that comprises all human lives; in fact, the very suggestion lacks authenticity. Each person does not discover but creates the world that he or she decides to live in. Imitation is not flattery but evinces a lack of personal choice regarding one's values, as if the choice of values itself was more important than the truth of them.

I was born into the transition period between these paradigms. With memories of 1950s television shows like *Leave It to Beaver* and *Father Knows Best* — pop Aristotelianism at its sentimental best — I was bewildered by the onset of the psychedelic sixties. After the Beatles broke up, I didn't have the stomach or the ear for the heavy metal phase that followed; it just sounded ugly to me. I started listening to classical music in 1971, Ravel and Debussy, and never looked back. Today my wife claims that, as a result of my musical bailout, I am a pop music illiterate. When we were married in the mideighties I took her Elton John records and threw them away. Yes, I got into trouble.

Highly sophisticated versions of the infatuation with subjectivity followed the sixties. Nietzsche was morphed into something called postmodernism, which basically announced the end of all objectivity, or what is called the logocentric view of the world. *Logos*, of course, is the Greek word for form or word and is used in the prologue to the Gospel of John to describe the second person of the Trinity, who become incarnate in Jesus Christ: "In the beginning was the Word...and the Word became flesh and dwelt among us."

If the world is not logocentric, then the Catholic Church is wrong. All Christians who accept the truth of the Scriptures believe that God created the world through the Word, and the Word's imprint and form is found everywhere in creation. "Through him all things were made." The world, the "out there" of our experience, is not an utterly alien thing — mysterious, yes, but mysterious in a way that can gradually reveal its depths and allow us to see into it. Mystery does not mean that something is unknowable; it means that knowing it requires time and patience, and that all that *can* be known will never *be* known, except to God.

Most people who are lost in their subjectivity have never heard of postmodernism or care about it. The advantage of knowing about postmodernism is that the choice becomes clear: you either create your standard for living, your notion of what it means to be a human being, or you discover it. The advantage of formal education is that the bad ideas that come with the air we breathe are made conscious and explicit. Most people given the chance to examine the assumptions that have led them into the hole of subjectivism will climb the ladder out. Others, liking the false sense of freedom, keep insisting, like Milton's

Satan, that it is better to be a leader than a follower, even if it leads to hell and unhappiness.

I was fortunate in my education for having teachers and friends who exposed me to fundamental questions. For example, my introduction to the world of philosophy came from the janitor in my high school, Arlington Heights High School in Fort Worth. While I was practicing the role of Peter in the senior play, *The Diary of Anne Frank,* I started talking to the janitor after rehearsals. He asked me if I had ever read Plato. No, I said, but I had heard about him and the way his teacher Socrates had been put to death. He said he was studying philosophy at a local college and lent me his beautiful Princeton University Press edition of Plato's dialogues, suggesting I read the *Apology* so we could discuss it the next night. I read it and was staggered by the story of a man willing to die when he could easily escape. Here was man more concerned about the integrity of serving his moral ideal than saving his own life.

After the rehearsal the next evening, the janitor began the conversation by asking me whether "existence precedes essence or essence existence." I said, "Well, how could there be any essence if there wasn't something to begin with, so existence must precede essence." With that we were off and running into a discussion that would last well into the night as we sat in the attic living room of the Frank family. Little did I know that janitor had introduced me to the very question — the primacy of existence — at the heart of the two philosophers whose work would lead me into the Church — Thomas Aquinas and Jacques Maritain.

Of course there is a subjective dimension to living in an objective world. You must choose to live *that way,* you must discover values and meaning with your own mind, and you must stay the course of your commitment to live well. These are difficult acts; they require effort and grace. Between what we see to do and what we can do is a gap that requires the power of God, the grace that comes through the sacraments. Get away from the sacraments and you find the vision growing remote and the power to reach it diminishing.

In the famous passage from book 7, section 9 of the *Confessions,* St. Augustine contrasts the difference between what he read in the Platonic philosophers and in the Gospels: in the Platonists Augustine read about the Word, but in Scripture he discovered the "Word became flesh and dwelt among us."

The Incarnation does more than show us the way. Christ empowers us as subjects, that is, you and me, to reach toward God, the objective goal of all our striving, the end of our desire for happiness. While claiming the meaning of things can be objectively known, the Church recognizes that all persons carry within themselves an inexhaustible depth of memory and aspiration. The sacraments are designed to envelope each individual in God's grace from the time of birth to the moment of death. Grace strengthens the interior life of every human being, as subject, to see, accept, and live out the values embedded in the nature of things, specifically, the nature of human life as created by God.

Objectivity is a great relief. Our culture is drowning in its preoccupation with feeling states. No wonder charismatics have grown in such great number over the past few decades. Professions of feelings have become the barometer of personal truth, the *summum bonum* of the search of happiness. And the more we care about feelings the more miserable we are.

Here is an irony I have witnessed over and over again: those who see the world and its values, including beauty, as objective, feel more deeply than those who profess that everything is subjective. Why? The reason is simple: in the world of the subjectivist even feelings have to be manufactured; they cannot be seen to be objectively elicited by something worthy of awe or wonder, because that would provide evidence for the presence of an objective form in the external world. No, even feelings are created by the sovereign individuals who paint the meaning of their world onto a blank canvas.

✢ *Six* ✢

STARTING WITH SOPHOCLES

R EADING AUGUSTINE made me dissatisfied with doing theology in the Baptist tradition, but I hadn't gone so far as pursuing any other. I had first started thinking about the Catholic Church during a lecture on Sophocles. The class was on religion and literature and the professor was a Roman Catholic priest, Rev. William F. Lynch, S.J.

Father Lynch was the first Catholic priest I had ever met. Growing up Protestant in Fort Worth, first as a Presbyterian and later as a Baptist, I was never in the proximity of anything remotely Catholic. So the day I first sat in a classroom staring at Father Lynch in his Roman collar was a strange one.

As a Southern Baptist, I had received all the standard warnings about Catholics: they are idolaters;

they worship Mary; they ignore the Bible. Since I never met any Catholics and was never forced to think about the tenets of their faith, I listened dutifully to what I was told, filing it away for later consideration. My decision to take a course from a Catholic priest, however, meant I couldn't ignore Catholicism any longer.

Lynch was a rather well known Jesuit, although his accomplishments as I read them on paper meant little to me. He was the editor of the journal *Thought*, then published at Fordham University, and the author of books such as *Christ and Apollo, Images of Faith, Christ and Prometheus*, and *Images of Hope*. Father Lynch, I would quickly realize, was equally conversant in theology, philosophy, psychology, and the arts, especially theater. But I knew almost nothing about his background when he began his first lecture on Sophocles' *Oedipus Rex.*

Like any dutiful undergraduate, I knew *Oedipus Rex* simply as a text to be read in translation from the ancient Greek. I assumed that any religious meaning in the drama should be gleaned from the speeches of its characters. Lynch, however, did not pay much attention to the text. Instead, he talked about the play from a director's viewpoint.

Father Lynch, we discovered, had once directed a stage version of the play. When we examined the scene in which Jocasta realizes she has married her own son Oedipus, Lynch was more interested in describing how he had lit the scene than in dissecting the lines themselves. He explained that this central moment of the play unfolds through the speech of a messenger while Jocasta herself remains silent. In his stage version, he put all the light on her face and left the rest of the stage in darkness, including the character speaking the lines that awaken her to her crime of incest.

Father Lynch treated the words as secondary: only the face of Jocasta really mattered. The truth she discovered in the voice of the messenger, telling of the child he released from bound feet, was registered in the horror on her face. Her face, her presence, carried the story of the play. In other words, what was being said had to take a step back so something could be shown. Lynch's lecture, for me, was an introduction to the meaning of presence, a foreshadowing of what I would one day know as sacramentality and *real* presence.

As I left the classroom, I wondered why his lecture had such a great impact on me. I had a hunch that it had something to do with the Catholic faith that expressed itself through him. As a Baptist, I was a minister of the spoken Word. The success or failure of a Baptist worship service is judged by the sermon and, as a confirmation, the number of those who walk the aisle in response. No wonder Baptists have such vitality in their preaching; no wonder they continue to produce preachers who can hold you spellbound. Baptist and evangelical preaching arguably has produced the only vital distinctive legacy of public speaking in the United States. One has only to listen to the southern senators to appreciate the vein of facility they are tapping.

Father Lynch himself was a small, frail man. There was nothing exotic or theatrical about him; he commanded attention simply by the force of his intelligence. I took the chance of befriending him, which he seemed to welcome. When word came in the middle of the semester that an illness would keep him from delivering any further lectures, I called him at the St. Ignatius of Loyola residence in Manhattan and asked if I could come by for a visit. I had no idea what kind of world I was about to step into. Entering the residence a few days later, I fully expected that Father Lynch's room would be filled with

Father William F. Lynch – "Father Lynch treated the words as secondary: only the face of Jocasta really mattered. . . . In other words, what was being said had to take a step back so something could be shown. Lynch's lecture, for me, was an introduction to the meaning of presence, a foreshadowing of what I would one day know as sacramentality and *real* presence."

the accoutrements of a man of learning and the arts: paintings would be hung on the walls, and bookcases filled to overflowing would line the rooms. Music, of course, would be wafting up from a record player, probably a string quartet.

When I knocked on the door, I heard a voice inviting me to enter. The living room was completely bare, with the exception of a few chairs and coffee table, and as I turned the corner into the bedroom I was stunned. Father Lynch lay in his bed, the only piece of furniture in the room except for a side table. Over his head was a crucifix, and in his hand was a copy of *Ulysses*. Nothing else was in sight. I don't remember much about the conversation; my mind was too busy trying to adjust to the simplicity of this man, and the juxtaposition of his faith and learning — the Crucified Christ and James Joyce. How did a Southern Baptist from Texas take this in? It took almost ten years.

I never saw Father Lynch again before he died, although I did talk to him on the phone when he agreed to write me a recommendation for graduate school in, yes, religion and literature.

The same year I met Father Lynch he published *Images of Faith: An Exploration of the Ironic Imagination*. The subject of Lynch's critique was Søren

Kierkegaard, perhaps the greatest of all nineteenth-century Protestant thinkers.

The irony of Kierkegaard's faith, as Lynch called it, was a faith always asserted against, or in spite of, the evidence. Kierkegaard's faith, thus, is always in a negative posture of looking beyond or behind the appearances of things, on the assumption that what is seen by human eyes cannot help lead to faith in "things unseen."

Lynch wrote that Kierkegaard's faith, "does not see.... It hears [the word of God or man]. It inserts this paradigm of hearing into its seeing, its imaging, its experiencing of the world."

I did not realize at the time that this was precisely the insight I had received in the midst of Father Lynch's Sophocles lecture. My "image" of faith had been challenged at a preconscious level: my faith was learning to see as well as to hear. My faith was beginning to acquire a body.

✢ Seven ✢

SOME
DISCONNECTS

THERE WERE ONLY A FEW graduate schools that offered a degree in theology and literature, so I was delighted when the Institute of the Liberal Arts at Emory University accepted me in its doctoral program.

When I arrived at Emory in the fall of 1974, one of the first people I met was a Cuban-American graduate student named Erasmo Leiva-Merikakis. Erasmo later became one of the leading translators and scholars of Hans Urs von Balthasar and authority on everything concerning the history of Catholicism and culture.

I asked Erasmo at the new student reception how he would describe himself. He told me he was a "Christian humanist," to which I replied in good

Baptist style, "Oh, 'Christian' is not good enough?" Rather than taking offense at the insolence of a young graduate student, he smiled brightly and said something to the effect that it was good to hear someone so outspoken about his faith.

Through Erasmo I was introduced to the greats of Catholic culture: the novelists (Evelyn Waugh, Julian Green, Graham Green, Georges Bernanos), the poets (Dante, Baudelaire, Rilke), the theologians (Henri de Lubac, Hans Urs von Balthasar, Yves Congar, Louis Bouyer, and Jean Daniélou). More importantly, perhaps, Erasmo, who had been a Trappist novice, introduced me to monastic spirituality. He took me to the Trappist monastery at Conyers, Georgia, to see the descendants of Flannery O'Connor's peacocks, to pray, and to sing chant with the monks. As we walked through the fields around the monastery Erasmo answered question after question I had concerning Mary. Later he would translate a book by von Balthasar on Mary, *The Threefold Garland.* The preface contains a sentence that reads, "This translation is dedicated to Deal Hudson, who asked me about Mary."

At that time, even though Catholicism was beginning to become more than an intellectual curiosity,

Erasmo Leiva-Merikakis – "I asked Erasmo at the new student reception how he would describe himself. He told me he was a 'Christian humanist,' to which I replied in good Baptist style, 'Oh, "Christian" is not good enough?'"

I was still trying to make it as a Southern Baptist minister. I took a job as an associate minister at Druid Hills Baptist Church. I met many wise and wonderful people at Druid Hills but began banging my head once again against the Baptist contempt for culture. My film nights, where I showed films like *Billy Budd* and *To Kill a Mockingbird,* incited complaints to the pastor from parents about how the youth minister was wasting their children's time.

So I found myself out of place in two different worlds. At Emory most viewed me as hopelessly backward: I was the Baptist from Texas trying to make sense of theological dimensions of literature without losing the primacy of revealed truth. At Druid Hills I was the young, arrogant Princeton graduate who didn't want to stay within the boundaries of *sola scriptura.*

Fortunately, my dissertation committee was made up of three men who, each in his own way, applauded my determination to uncover linkages between the Christian faith and culture. David Hesla, my advisor, the son of a Lutheran minister and a practicing Episcopalian, showed me the ways of Aristotle's *Poetics* as the key to discerning the moral content of great literature. Arthur Evans, a devout Catholic who had taught at the University of Notre Dame, often invited me to sit in his backyard, drink tea, and discuss the spirituality of poets and novelists. Don Saliers, a Methodist theologian, introduced me to the liturgical understanding of both theology and literature. I couldn't have found three better men, three better Christian teachers, to open the door to the Church.

Thus it was no great surprise when I chose a theologian, a poet, and a philosopher — namely, Kierkegaard, Baudelaire, and Nietzsche — for my dissertation on antiromanticism. My dissertation, in retrospect, was my attempt, using Protestant assumptions, to overcome the barriers between faith and culture. Instead, I reached a dead end. I didn't know it at the time, but later on, when I began reading Thomas Aquinas seriously, the inadequacy of my methodology and metaphysical assumptions became clear.

After I received my doctorate in 1979, my first job offer came from Metropolitan Baptist Church, then the only Southern Baptist church in Manhattan. When I went to "preach in view of a call," I chose as my sermon text the story by Flannery O'Connor "A Good Man Is Hard to Find." I thought the literary angle would appeal to the cosmopolitan Baptists of the Big Apple.

I noticed as I was preaching that my congregation seemed rather perplexed. Their faces grew even more puzzled when I finished my sermon by emphasizing the famous scene at the end of the story in which the Misfit shoots the grandmother and says, "She would have been a good woman if it had been somebody there to shoot her every minute of her life." My gloss on that text seemed as obvious to me then as it does now — that all of us become better people when we face the fact of our own mortality. When nobody came down the aisle during the invitation, I assumed my audition was a flop.

Later that night in my room at the Edison Hotel across from Lincoln Center the phone rang and the chairman of the search committee — much to my surprise — offered me the job. I asked him if I could sleep on it. That night, with the sound of the elevator keeping me awake, I realized I could not in good conscience accept, because, intellectually, I had become a Catholic. I went back to Atlanta with no prospects of a job.

Though I had left Druid Hills a year earlier, the Baptists had not given up on me yet. With resumé in hand I called on the dean of Mercer University in Atlanta, Dr. Jean Hendricks. She had no regular

Flannery O'Connor – "I chose as my sermon text the story by Flannery O'Connor, 'A Good Man Is Hard to Find.' I thought the literary angle would appeal to the cosmopolitan Baptists of the Big Apple."

teaching slots available but asked me if I would like to teach humanities courses to inmates at the state and federal penitentiaries. Under the inspired guidance of Dean Hendricks I learned the trade of teaching in the Mercer prison program. I spent the next year teaching ethics, religion, literature, and music appreciation inside barbed wired fences and cell blocks. There was no better place in the world for me to learn the art and the grandeur of being a teacher.

✢ Eight ✢

DEFENDING
WOMAN

IN THE LAST THREE MONTHS of 1979, I had finished my dissertation, turned down the pastor's
job in New York City, and accepted the teaching
post offered by Dr. Hendricks. My dissertation had
focused on romanticism as seen by later nineteenth-
century critics — Søren Kierkegaard, Charles Baudelaire, and Friedrich Nietzsche. In particular, I used
Kierkegaard's critique of the aesthetic life to expose
the limitations of Wordsworth, Coleridge, Novalis,
Chateaubriand, and other early nineteenth-century
romantics. My devotion to Kierkegaard became, as I
see it now, the final struggle to defend my Protestant
faith against the lure of beauty and all that it entails.

You might say the dissertation was a success: I
used Kierkegaard to slay the dragons of romantic

excess, its indiscriminate yearnings, its impatience with suffering and finitude. I enlisted Nietzsche and the Catholic poet Baudelaire — in Kierkegaardian guise — as allies in my polemic. But as I finished the final chapter I knew something was wrong. I had noticed a common failing in all three of my protagonists, a failing that manifested itself in their attitudes toward women, or should I say, woman?

I wrote an additional chapter, one that had not been part of the original outline, entitled "The Isolation of the Self." I noted that each of my subjects not only lived isolated from society and family but wrote about women as obstacles to their sense of vocation — Baudelaire as poet, Nietzsche as philosopher, and Kierkegaard as Christian. None of these men had satisfying relationships with women, and none of them ever married. Kierkegaard famously arranged for his fiancé, Regina Olsen, to break off her engagement to him so to avoid inflicting his melancholy suffering on her or allowing her domestic demands to undermine his heroic effort to live as a Christian. He often opined that just the fact of being married was an obstacle to being a Christian.

Baudelaire kept a mistress, Jeanne Duval, on and off for nearly twenty years, but she seems to have been more of a tormenting muse and financial burden than a lover. The poet was disgusted when his "white Venus," the beautiful Madame Sabatier, offered herself to him sexually after receiving from him some of the greatest love poems written in the French language. He wrote to Sabatier, "A few days ago you were a divinity, which is so convenient, so beautiful, so inviolable. Now you are a woman...."

Nietzsche, who said, "When you go to a woman take a whip," proposed to Lou Salome several times, but, after her continued rejections, become forever embittered toward women. He writes in *Genealogy of Morals* of women's bodies and his desire for them as an obstacle to philosophy: "The philosopher abhors marriage, together with what might persuade to it.... What great philosopher hitherto has been married?"

I concluded that the reason each of these "antiromantics," as I called them, still suffered from the isolation of the romantic heroes they despised was that they were playing out the dynamics of a problematic age. Little did I realize that the struggles I uncovered in them were my own. In surveying their view of woman I was taking on much larger issues connected with the real presence, the maternity of

Mary, the sacramentality of creation, and the beauty of God. One day, kneeling before a picture of Mary in an Atlanta parish, I realized how much of my own fear of God's presence I had played out intellectually in these figures.

I'm puzzled by those who accuse the Catholic Church of showing a lack of respect to women. For someone coming from the evangelical tradition, I see that the feminine dimensions of Catholicism are found everywhere. Evangelicalism being so closely wedded to the spoken word also comes across as strongly masculine. The femininity of Catholicism is captured, though far from exhausted by, the figure of Mary and her Magnificat — "My soul magnifies the Lord" — not by speaking or by great exterior struggles but by the simple presence of the Mother who loves her child before everything else. The passionate attention that Mary pays to her son, Jesus, is reflected throughout Catholic worship and spirituality, especially in the Church's respect for silence and eucharistic adoration.

Baudelaire, Nietzsche, and Kierkegaard shared a fear of otherness, and woman was its metaphor. At the core of their discomfort was a fear of physical presence. For each of them, woman was symbolic of that not-self in which society is seen as fundamentally antagonistic. The pressure of their physical presence, heightened by their beauty and the erotic desire it elicited, manifested as obstacles to be overcome rather than partners in spiritual growth. Why? Because, as Father Lynch might have put it, woman had to be overcome by an ironic journey into the self. Kierkegaard put it bluntly in *Training in Christianity* when he claimed that fellowship is a lower category than the lone individual. If the individual loses integrity by virtue of entering community, then maintenance of selfhood requires isolation. All human love, he seems to be agreeing with Freud, is fundamentally self-love.

Where else is one to go? If not toward the other, the only recourse is toward the self, the self as creative, overcoming, or believing. In each act, the self carries the burden of inventing meaning and happiness in the face of an alien, fallen world, where the intended helpmate of man, the woman, is a permanent impediment. The contrast with the figure of Mary as giving birth to the Savior could not be more startling.

How did I ever get out of this corner? I was spiritually and intellectually at the crossroads.

✤ *Nine* ✤

TEACHING
THE ABSOLUTE

M Y FIRST CLASS as a college professor was a
course on philosophical ethics at the state
penitentiary in Gainesville, Georgia. Was it naiveté
that made me confident in assigning Plato's *Apology*, Aristotle's *Ethics*, and Augustine's *Confessions* as
the texts for the class? Our classroom was the prison
weight room. I sat on the bench press while my dozen
students, eleven African American men in jail for
drugs and one white male for killing his wife, sat on
folding chairs in a semicircle.

I spent most of my first year of teaching either at
the state or federal penitentiary, offering everything
from introductory philosophy to religion and music
appreciation. Perhaps nothing exposes the preten-
sions of a young professor more than inmate students.

66

I learned very quickly that they wanted to know the bottom line, about my subjects and about me.

The first few classes seemed to go well. But at the beginning of the second week, during a discussion of virtue in Aristotle I noticed some giggling and whispering among them. I asked what was up and was surprised to get such a straight answer: "We think that anyone who talks about things like virtue and morality is only trying to deceive other people into trusting him so he can make money."

"So all of you think all discussion of morality is really about making an impression, nothing more?" One by one they told me that they didn't believe anyone was really interested in doing good when nobody was watching. I told them I would have to sleep on their question.

I went home rather shaken by the question they raised and the fact that all of them were so cynical about ethics. This particular angle had not come up in any classroom I could remember. But it did expose a weakness in the teaching of morality. The notion that being virtuous is never harming another person limits the idea of a good life to how one relates to someone else, and it leaves oneself completely out. After all, isn't every acting individual a person and every person affected by his or her own actions? I devised a scenario to force my students to think about the moral relationship one has to oneself. Perhaps if they could see that being ethical was in their own interest? I was reasoning from natural law even though the phrase was not familiar to me at the time. Aristotle prepared me for my reading of Aquinas and Maritain by showing that the proper focus of ethics was human nature, specifically those habits and acts that fulfill the human potential for reaching its end of happiness.

At the next class I asked them to imagine they lived on a desert island where they had all the basic goods they needed to live: food, shelter, and moderate weather. But there were no other people, and there was no God. I wanted a situation where the only person around was oneself. Since there was no one to act toward, then they would have to consider how they would treat themselves. I then asked whether they would consider it good or evil to wake up one morning and decide to cut off a hand. All the students but one, the convicted murderer, quickly announced, "Sure, what's wrong with that if I want to?" I argued that cutting off a hand was an evil against oneself, against the healthy body that enables one to live fully. Sure, I said, you are able to cut off your hand, but just the ability to do something doesn't make it right.

That line of argument quickly led to using drugs, which all of them did even in prison: their glassy eyes sometimes testified to the ease with which drugs were smuggled over the high chain link fence. During the discussion a few came around, at least for the moment, to admit that they deserved to be treated well, as a person that is, even by *their own actions*. Like most people used to throwing about the word "rights," my students identified a right with anything they had the hankering to do.

They seemed to appreciate that I had struggled with their question from the previous class, and one of them decided to do for me what he considered a favor. He stopped me in the hall during the bathroom break and asked me how much money I made teaching philosophy. When I told him I was being paid $10,000 he laughed and told me I could be making much more, about $5,000 a month more. "Look, you have students all around you at the college, right? Why don't you let my contacts supply you with drugs and you sell them to your students?"

"No, I can't do that," I replied.

His eyes looked hurt at my answer. "You're a good guy, we all like you here, and you should be making more money. This will be easy for you."

"As much as I like the money, there are some things I just can't do, and selling drugs is one of them."

"You don't use drugs?" He seemed incredulous.

"No, I don't. They never appealed to me."

He laughed again as he went into class muttering something about letting him know if I changed my mind.

Driving back to Atlanta that night I realized that there really is a self-esteem component to education, even though I often made fun of those who talked about it. My inmate students didn't care what happened to themselves by their own hand. Perhaps it's better to say they lacked self-love because they didn't need to be any fonder of themselves, in an emotional sense, than they already were. What they lacked was real caring about the real good for themselves, a good that opposed evils like the drugs they caught as they were thrown over the back fence in paper bags.

The great critic George Steiner once said that teachers are "postmen for the absolute," and that day in that class was my first and best lesson in how difficult that is. Though I learned a lesson I never forgot, one that I drew upon during my fifteen years of teaching, I doubt if any of them would remember me or those days in class.

The following summer I offered my first course on the philosophy of love at Mercer University Atlanta. It dealt with a number of ethical questions arising from the nature of family life, including abortion, contraception, and euthanasia. In those days, at a small Baptist college you could ask your students where they stood on these questions without fear of class meltdown.

On the day we discussed abortion I was stunned into silence by one student's explanation of why she, as a mother, supported abortion: "I believe in abortion because I love children." I wanted to scream out, "How can love cause you to kill another human being, an unborn child?" Once I recovered my composure, I probed her on the meaning of the word "love" as she had just used it. She explained that aborting an unborn child who was being born to a mother who did not want the child, did not want to care for the child, would save the child from suffering. So love, for her, protects someone from suffering, even if it deprives that person of existence itself.

Doesn't existence precede essence, precede suffering, and precede everything? Isn't life good and to be welcomed, regardless of suffering?

Indeed the question posed to me as a high school senior kept coming up under all kinds of different guises, especially in the midst of ethical arguments. In this case, a mother believes she is being sensitive in wishing the death of the child so the child can avoid suffering. So she applies an ideal, an essence, to a life, an existence, and finds it wanting, so the life can be ended because it does not live up to the ideal. That is a classic example of how essence cannot precede existence or all essences lose their mooring in what is really real, existence itself.

To put essence prior to existence is to invent a wholly new world in accord with your individual wishes or the wishes of some group you want to please or belong to. Usually such projects have lofty goals, such as the creation of a more perfect world or the elimination of injustice or inequality. The reason these projects fail or turn into oppression is that the ideals that inspire them are so far removed from the human existence they wish to guide.

Jacques Maritain talked about the "intuition of being," a moment when an individual undergoes the sudden awareness that the fact of existence precedes oneself and all one's reflection about it. These intuitions have been hotly debated among scholars of St. Thomas, but whether they can be used philosophically is less important than whether they occur. And I believe they do. They can occur in the midst of human encounters, while enjoying works of art, or walking alone in the woods.

At the heart of the intuition of being is the certainty that though my self is the source of my consciousness, it is not the originator of either the power of consciousness or the world it seeks to know. Something drives and sustains my self and the world, which join together in my reflection. All that I am is encompassed.

Rather than making the world, we receive it. From the perspective of the absolute, we are passive recipients of being. As such, existence should be the occasion of gratitude, and of a sense of obligation to learn its laws and protect the life it bestows. Scripture gives us revealed laws, such as the Ten Commandments, to guide our actions and instruct us in the virtues. But the Catholic tradition recognizes that nature is also a teacher, and the laws taught by nature are in harmony with those taught by revelation. The advantage of revealed law is its certainty and clarity; the advantage of natural law is its availability to all human minds and the broadness of its application.

These classroom encounters even led me to offer a series of classes on the subject of love and happiness and to my book *Happiness and the Limits of Satisfaction*. That book, ten years in the making, brought happiness as conceived by Aristotle and Aquinas into conversation with the psychological view of happiness that has dominated thinking since the nineteenth century. The mother who kills her child to protect the child from predictable suffering places more value on the importance of positive psychological states than anything else. The inmate justifying self-mutilation on the grounds of personal preference makes the same mistake. When a happy life is understood as nothing more than a series of pleasant, positive feeling states, then it's no surprise that drug use and other methods of pain avoidance are widely used and indulged. Unrealizable and destructive ideals about life are employed to measure the way life should be lived.

In reading books on happiness written throughout history I noticed that Catholic writers were the least likely to make this mistake. They understood, perhaps from the example of Christ himself or from the great saints, that the most admirable lives usually exhibited the mark of great suffering, even martyrdom. If a happy life is the best life, the one we would be most likely to admire and emulate, then suffering must be accepted. Catholics also have the advantage of being deeply influenced by the classical philosophers who make the attainment of virtue — beneficial habits of character — a necessary condition of a happy life.

I sought to capture what Catholics learned about happiness from the suffering of Christ and the saints by describing the "passion of happiness." These are odd words to place together in the contemporary climate of happiness as self-congratulation. Passion has the generic meaning of being acted upon, as opposed to being active. Lovers are passionate in the sense that their mutual attraction overwhelms them and spurs them to intense action. But passion begins with something that happens to you, something that comes upon you. The first thing that comes to all of us is our life, the fact that we exist. We did not create the world we live in, no matter how hard we seek to re-create it in our minds or on paper in theoretical constructs.

The passion of happiness begins in sheer gratitude and love for life and the One who created it. All the acts and habits that flow from that love become the moral core of a life lived well and worthy to be judged as being happy. It's typical of the consonance between the classical and Catholic traditions that judgments about who was happy were made by third parties. In other words, persons did not judge their own happiness because it was not a matter of reading their own psychological states: it was their character that mattered, and that could be judged by others.

✣ Ten ✣

THE BIRD SINGS

THE YEAR I SPENT teaching in the prison program along with my first reading of Aristotle's
Ethics left me hungering for an entirely new direction for my scholarly and personal research. I had
lost interest in pursuing the Christian ironies and
dialectics of Kierkegaard that had guided me through
my dissertation. I was looking for a new place to start.

I had come home one day from class and had
the afternoon free. I wanted to read something different, entirely different. So I picked out a red
paperback volume of the first thirteen questions of
the *Summa* (the Blackfriars edition edited by Thomas
Gilby, O.P.) from my bookshelf, one I had had since
seminary, but never read.

It was spring, so I put a chair in the backyard
and began at the beginning. It took a few pages

to figure out how to read Thomas's strange mini-disputations, called "articles," and after I stopped getting the argument backward I was soon engrossed.

Reading through the questions on the simplicity and perfection of God, I realized that I was starting to look at God and the world in a wholly new way. But when I came to the question: "Is everything that exists good?" my attention was suddenly riveted.

His answer begins: "Anything that exists is either God or created by God. Now every creature of God is good, says St. Paul. And God himself is supremely good. So everything that exists is good" (Ia, 5, 3, sed contra). I knew instantly I had found the answer I had been looking for, a way past the dead end of my dissertation. I didn't know all the whys and where-fores of this answer as an answer. All I knew was that this simple assertion of St. Thomas supplied a foundation that I had been missing, both in my faith and in my reasoning.

"Everything that exists is good." Here is a foun-dation of goodness in creation that could not be destroyed either by my personal sinfulness or by the disasters and tragedies that befall us. This goodness was derived from an inexhaustible font of goodness. It was a goodness that extended beyond the seemingly safe parameters of my self and all selves and made the presence of the world to my senses, to my mind, and to my heart a good thing. Not only was I was caught up in the arms of God from the very fact that I was, but all that was present to me through the windows of sense also bore witness to God's goodness.

At that moment something happened that confirmed this insight through the senses themselves. I was sitting beneath a tree and a bird feeder. A redbird had arrived for a feeding while I'd been struggling with the scholastic setting of Aquinas's articles. As I turned that phrase over and over in my mind, "everything that exists is good," the redbird began to sing and somehow that phrase was taken up into the bird's song, and for a moment (I don't know how long) the bird was singing the saint's words, the words and the song were one and the same thing.

I am not a mystic, and I am not prone to out-of-body experiences, but that day — the day of the vision and the song — has marked the rest of my life. With that single idea Aquinas set me on the final road to conversion and confirmation. He saved me from the fate of my three antiromanticists who sought in a highly cultivated world of self-consciousness what they doubted could be discovered in the world of the senses.

The new freedom I felt was real; I now knew that the lure of beauty was part of God's own providence, that the delight of his creation and his artists reflected the inexhaustible reserve of God's own life.

So here I was — thirty years old, Ph.D. in hand, teaching the humanities for a Baptist college to prisoners, and, because of the *Summa Theologiae* of Thomas Aquinas, I was finally on my way to becoming a Catholic. What was going to happen to me?

I confided in Dr. Hendricks, the dean at Mercer University, that I wanted to explore my growing interest in Catholicism, and she bought me a ticket to visit Erasmo at the St. Ignatius Institute at the University of San Francisco. During that trip I taught a class for the founder of Ignatius Press, Dr. Joseph Fessio, jogged with him along the Presidio, and ate lunch on the pier at Sausalito with the French theologian Father Louis Bouyer.

Bouyer was in residence at the St. Ignatius Institute that semester. His book *The Spirit and Forms of Protestantism* had answered several lingering questions from my Baptist understanding of the Catholic faith. Did Catholics really reject the primacy of Scripture as the revelation of God's truth (the principle of *sola scriptura*)? Did Catholics substitute good works

Louis Bouyer – "Bouyer laughed as he told me the story of writing this book, which was his doctoral dissertation at the University of Strasbourg. 'I was a Lutheran when I started it and Catholic when I finished it.'"

for faith, thus minimizing the justifying death and resurrection of Christ (*sola gratia*)? Did Catholics put their own understanding of tradition ahead of the belief in the Bible (*sola fidei*)?

Bouyer's book shows that these principles have always been part of the Catholic tradition. They were not invented by Luther or Calvin and their spiritual descendants. In the Catholic tradition these principles are given primacy, rather than being treated as an either/or proposition: either grace or works, grace or nature, tradition or Scripture. "The main error of Protestantism lies in this, that it has come to associate inseparably, but quite artificially, the positive statements of the Reformation with certain negations, so that these have come to seem equally characteristic of its nature" (*The Spirit and Forms of Protestantism*).

The primacy of faith, justification, and Scripture does not negate the role of reason, virtue, or tradition. Bouyer calls these "fictitious oppositions." Indeed, as he shows, Scripture itself exposes the false dichotomy that Protestants affirm. Tradition precedes Scripture, a historical fact that evangelicals hate being reminded of. Without a tradition that preserves the Word of God from age to age, believers are cut off from the Body of Christ: "The final result is that the Protestant who seeks, in his Church, food for his faith finds it only in the form of total subjection to all the peculiarities, the momentary idiosyncrasies of his minister's personal devotion."

Bouyer laughed as he told me the story of writing this book, which was his doctoral dissertation at the University of Strasbourg. "I was a Lutheran when I started it and Catholic when I finished it."

In addition to my visits with Fessio and Bouyer, I was led without much warning to the front door of a Carmelite monastery.

✠ *Eleven* ✠

MY NUN STORY

I WENT TO SAN FRANCISCO for answers, intellectual ones, to questions about the Catholic Church. I looked forward to sitting at the feet of Louis Bouyer, walking and talking with Erasmo, and seeing first-hand the good work of Father Joseph Fessio, S.J., at newly founded St. Ignatius Press.

But I was surprised when Erasmo said he had made an appointment for me to meet the Carmelite nuns who lived in a monastery down the street from his house. He said they were expecting me the next morning at 10:00 a.m. I was surprised and upset when he said he wasn't going with me.

I thought to myself that the visit was getting out of hand. Yes, I had made this trip to San Francisco to talk about Catholicism. Yes, I was interested. But talking to nuns all by myself in a convent? That seemed a bit extreme — like throwing a five-year-old in the deep end of the pool to teach him how to swim. I pressed him to go with me but Erasmo assured me that I was expected.

I had no idea how to visit with nuns or what to say to them. I had admired the idea of nuns but had never thought you could actually talk to them, especially when they lived behind high stone walls. I was embarrassed at my sense of ineptitude.

When Erasmo left me at the front door of the convent I thought of various excuses for not keeping the appointment. I could say, "I don't think my level of interest in faith merits an actual face-to-face meeting with . . . nuns!" Or, "Is it a good idea for a man who likes sex to visit nuns who have no sex?"

I knew at the time that they were lame excuses, but I couldn't find any real point in my visit to the nuns down the street beyond making Erasmo happy. I guess that was going to be a good enough reason to get me through this awkward moment — knocking on the door of a convent.

The convent door was massive and looked as if it hadn't been opened for years. Erasmo pointed to the bell chain, said, "I'll see you around noon at the chapel," and walked away without showing any awareness that I wanted to run away.

I stood on the corner for a few minutes since it wasn't yet ten o'clock. I looked at cars passing on the street, the men and women walking by, and felt a sudden burst of pride in being a young man on holiday in a great city, with nothing to do but enjoy myself.

Turning around to the convent door I felt sorry for those nuns inside — they were shut off from this feeling, this elation of freedom and youth. I then realized why I should go inside and meet the nuns. They needed visitors like me, I thought. They must be lonely for company, someone who talks to them about the beauty of being out in the world. After all, they probably don't have a television, and I doubt that they read the newspaper and watch movies.

I can't believe I talked myself into thinking that my visit would be good for them, such was my naiveté and pride at the time. I thought of myself as a handsome visitor from the outside bringing them news from the world. I could pull the chain because I was confident in my new role. As I expected, it was a while before it opened. I was greeted not by a nun but by a Hispanic housemaid who pointed to a wooden chair to the right of the door as I entered.

Looking around I saw nothing except the chair facing a wall and a doorway to the left through which the housemaid disappeared. I sat in the chair and looked at the wall, noticing it contained some kind of finely designed wooden windows, like the ticket windows of a Victorian opera house.

I sat a while wondering if I should walk around and explore the room, but there was really nothing else to see except a few examples of Catholic kitsch on the walls.

So I sat contentedly thinking of how I would entertain the sisters with stories about myself, particularly why I was in the city visiting my friend on a kind of religious quest. I assumed they would be eager to hear all I had to say, and it would be a nice break from the routine of their day inside the walls of the convent.

I began to hear something padding softly across the floor behind the wall in front of me. Then the windows started to rattle and slide to the side. Suddenly there were two nun faces in front of me, an older one and a younger one. The younger introduced herself as the novice mistress, and the other, she explained, was the prioress of the convent. The prioress started to speak, but I was already taken aback — they didn't appear bored by their life behind the walls, or excited at the prospect of a few minutes with a young man from outside.

They were beautiful, in fact — both of them. To this day I don't think I have seen more beautiful faces. It was confusing. What was coming from behind the wall, through the window, felt more vibrant than the street corner I had stood upon a few minutes earlier.

How could these nuns be so beautiful, so happy? I wondered. Somewhere in the midst of our conversation I blurted out this awkward question.

Their laugh reminded me of the way the good witch laughs in *The Wizard of Oz* when Dorothy whines that she'll never see Kansas again.

The explanation made me suddenly jealous of their lives: where I had previously seen only restrictions and huge stone walls, I now saw the freedom of simplicity. They told me about the privilege they enjoyed of spending their days in prayer and work. Life, they said, was so much more difficult outside the walls, and their job was to pray for others, for those who were not as blessed as they were.

They asked me about my struggles and my suffering. Their questions were posed so innocently that I took absolutely no offense at their prying into my personal life. In fact, the question itself seemed to lance a boil in my soul, and the pain poured out, not in a torturous explanation, but in a simple explanation. Their presence seemed to make me less pretentious and more able to talk about myself without adding layers of explication.

Talk about the tables turning! When they offered to pray for me I knew I was getting a real gift, something much more than the usual "our thoughts will be with you" variety.

It's one thing to get intellectual answers, quite another for holiness to smack you across the face. The next time I would see holiness like this was at a private Mass in the Vatican with John Paul II. When I walked into his chapel and saw him kneeling before the altar, with his massive back slumped into prayer, I once again experienced how sanctity itself puts the mind to rest. After all, isn't this the reason for all the questions, all the restless reflections? The point is to get somewhere, and that place is holiness, to love and to be loved by God perfectly. In seeing the nuns, as in seeing the Holy Father, knowledge comes all at once in a kind of vision, an intuition of all that we are seeking. The beauty of holiness answers all questions by placing the goal of our desire before our eyes.

This may explain why St. Thomas Aquinas stopped working on his *Summa Theologiae* months before his unexpected death at age forty-nine. When asked by his secretary why he had stopped his dictation, Aquinas responded, "All I have written seems to me nothing but straw...compared to what I have seen and what has been revealed to me."

When I am asked what nuns do to help the world, I simply say, "They pray for us. What's more helpful than that?" Those who pray and who understand the power of prayer understand without further explanation. (Often the evangelical is the first to understand.)

When the window closed and they padded away, I felt that someone had turned the lights off. Outside the convent walls the street seemed a lot less glamorous than before.

As I walked toward the chapel at the University of San Francisco to meet Erasmo, I kept seeing their faces framed by the black and white cloth of their habits. I wondered if they would be as beautiful if they were living in the world. Probably not, I decided — too many worries, too much trouble.

No one was at the chapel when I arrived. I stood around for a while, thinking I had to do the right thing: what was the right thing to do before Mass and after visiting with nuns?

I took the opportunity when no one was looking to dip my fingers in the holy water and make the sign of the cross over my head and chest. I had always wanted to try that, but it seemed so superstitious.

I turned around to make sure no one was watching and caught Erasmo smiling at me.

✢ Twelve ✢

A LETTER FROM
ST. LOUIS

WITHIN A FEW MONTHS of returning from San
Francisco in the spring of 1980 I received a
large cardboard box with the words "Catholic Bomb"
written across the top. Erasmo had sent me my required reading. I dutifully studied the books he sent,
but some of them made me take a few steps backward
from conversion.

I began to notice many negative references to
the Second Vatican Council (1962–65). Books like
Maritain's *Peasant of the Garonne* (1967) and James
Hitchcock's *Catholicism & Modernity* (1979) raised
serious questions about the long-term impact of the
"spirit" of Vatican II — not the sixteen documents of
the council itself — on the character of the Catholic
Church.

The significance of the council for the future of the Church had evidently been hijacked by Catholic journalists and academics eager to challenge and change the structure of ecclesial authority and, especially, to countermand the teaching of Pope Paul VI's subsequent encyclical *Humane Vitae* (1967), which upheld the Church's ban against contraception.

During the late 1970s and early 1980s, when I was reading most intensely, these dissident voices were at their height, marking a public victory by winning the tenure battle of Dr. Charles Curran at the Catholic University of America. Unknown to me at the time were the efforts of frustrated Catholic laymen and priests who were organizing a defense of Church teaching, such as the founding of *Crisis* magazine, first called *Crisis in Catholicism*, in 1982 by Ralph McInerny and Michael Novak.

The Vatican II documents had been sitting on my shelves for quite a while, but I decided it was time to read them for myself, all of them. As I did, none of my fears was realized, because the sixteen documents bore no resemblance to their reputation among dissenting theologians. Indeed I was struck at how traditional they were, in the best sense. They were truly an *aggiornamento*, an updating, of Catholic liturgy and doctrine, not an overturning or overhauling. They were great essays in theology, somehow collectively written, and obviously of a piece with the theological tradition I had come to embrace first through St. Augustine and then through St. Thomas, Maritain and other later Thomists, von Balthasar, and de Lubac.

I couldn't detect any connection in spirit or substance between what I was seeing played out among Catholic dissenters cheering on Professor Curran in the "name of Vatican II" and what was found in these documents. I have had occasion over the years to reread them several times, and I am still impressed by their clarity in presenting the relationship of authority between the Holy Father and his bishops.

"The college or body of bishops has for all that no authority unless united with the Roman Pontiff, Peter's successor, as its head, whose primatial authority, let it be added, over all, whether pastors or faithful, remains in its integrity. For the Roman Pontiff, by reason of his office as Vicar of Christ, namely, as pastor of the entire Church, has full, supreme and universal power over the whole Church, a power which he can always exercise unhindered" (*Lumen Gentium* 22).

Still perplexed, however, by what was being said and done in the Church under the aegis of Vatican II, I wrote to historian James Hitchcock of St. Louis University. I asked him a blunt question: why should I, a Protestant, join the Catholic Church if it is becoming Protestant, as you seem to imply in your book? To this day I am mindful to return phone calls, e-mails, and letters (though I don't always succeed) because of the importance of his letter in response to me. Hitchcock had complained in his book about the fewer number of converts to the Church after the council; perhaps he was taken aback by this letter from a young enthusiast for all the things he thought had been forgotten — Maritain, Aquinas, Newman, and the rest. Dated January 25, 1980, the letter reads in part:

"Thanks very much for your letter. I understand rather acutely, I think, the dilemma you find yourself in. I am sometimes embarrassed for my church in its present failings.

"I think my basic answer to your questions would be to say that when one becomes a Catholic one in effect enters into unity with the Church in its widest sense — not only the geographical breadth that exists at present but also all the ages which have gone before.

To enter the Catholic Church because of an affinity with Newman, et al., is quite legitimate, because the tradition of the Church is broad and deep and is implicitly carried along to each new age.

"A certain historical-mindedness is a great advantage for a Catholic, hence being a scholar is also an advantage. However, for the religious clay one finds in one's local community, one can always travel across the centuries to enter in unity with the great saints and theologians.

"At the present time one would also have to distinguish, I think, between the local church and the universal church. On the local level what one finds is often discouraging. (Obviously if you are in a large city you have more to choose from.) Without wanting to be quoted on it I would also say that the national leadership of the Catholic Church in this country is rather undistinguished — well-meaning but timid and confused men.

"Clearly, however, it is not the case with the Pope, and I believe he will have a significant impact on the Church in the next twenty years. Again, with regard to Roman Catholicism, it is legitimate to prescind from conditions at the local level in order to assert unity with the center. This is not an evasion or a rationalization — it is the reality of the Catholic concept of the Church.

"In a sense I may be talking out of both sides of my mouth. On one level we may say that the Church is concrete and visible. But on another level I seem to be proposing a kind of mystical unity that obliterates inconvenient specific realities. I think authentic Catholicism requires both. We are very insistent on the concrete and visible, but we do understand it in the widest sense. We are part of the stream of Catholic tradition, and we know what a lot of debris gets picked up along the way. We give our allegiance to a visible Church, but also know that ultimately our unity there is mystical."

How right Hitchcock was to predict the impact of John Paul II and his long pontificate!

Hitchcock's letter hit the nail on the head; he said just what I needed to hear at the time: the Church is not the church. The Church is an objective, supernatural reality united with history. His letter led me to further reading on the distinction between the historical Church and the mystical body of Christ, particularly in the work of Henri de Lubac. In *The Splendor of the Church*, de Lubac writes:

"The Bride of Christ cannot be degraded.... Her doctrine remains perpetually pure and the spring of her sacraments perpetually fresh.... Throughout the whole body of the Church, this treasure is always a variable quantity. The effects of grace vary in intensity from age to age and soul to soul, and we can never judge them with certainty. Sanctity sometimes flowers more profusely and sometimes more intensely, sometimes in brilliance and sometimes in secret.... In this world the Church is a mixed community and will stay like that to the very end — unthreshed corn, the ark with both clean and unclean animals, a ship full of unruly passengers who always seem to be on the point of wrecking it."

With the help of Hitchcock and de Lubac, I began to see more clearly how the Church can be both secure in its "sacred deposit of faith" and still suffer periods of decline and decadence. The Church really is "the thing" that Chesterton once called it, a reality that was established by the life and death of Christ and made present to all souls, regardless of their beliefs. The Church is always there, not so much behind the sin and dissent but in its very midst!

Vatican II, as a pastoral council, attempted to undo some of the abuse of those who took the objectivity of the Church for granted, those who had given up trying to make the Church accessible to the young and to the adult convert. Just because it's true and good doesn't mean that the Church can ignore its beauty, and the possibilities of that beauty for instruction and inspiration.

In October 1992, on the thirtieth anniversary of Vatican II, John Paul II wrote the following words as an introduction to the revised *Catechism of the Catholic Church:* "The principal task entrusted to the Council by Pope John XXIII was to guard and present better the precious deposit of Christian doctrine in order to make it more accessible to the Christian faithful and to all people of good will. For this reason the Council was not first of all to condemn the errors of the time, but above all to strive calmly to show the strength and beauty of the doctrine of faith."

Like most attempts at finding a new balance between old and new, much of the new liturgy since Vatican II has been less than beautiful, to put it politely. Rewording pop songs and equipping strolling liturgists with cordless microphones have seemingly solved the problem of connecting with the congregation. But few and far between are the parishes whose liturgies embody what Vatican II envisioned.

James Hitchcock – "With the help of Hitchcock and de Lubac, I began to see more clearly how the Church can be both secure in its 'sacred deposit of faith' and still suffer periods of decline and decadence."

"The treasury of sacred music is to be preserved and cultivated with great care. Choirs must be assiduously developed, especially in cathedral churches. Bishops and other pastors of souls must take great care to ensure that whenever the sacred action is to be accompanied by chant, the whole body of the faithful may be able to contribute that active participation which is rightly theirs" (*Sacrosanctum Concilium* 114).

But Catholics still go to Mass because they believe God is present to them there, and, knowing that, they perceive a beauty that cannot be spoiled by the bungling efforts to "connect" with them. Catholics exhibit a patient acquiescence at Mass rather than the celebration that should be the norm.

I recall the class on music appreciation I taught at the federal penitentiary in Atlanta. For the class on Renaissance polyphony I played two compositions. The first was by Tomás Luis de Victoria, the motet *Magnum Mysterium*, surely one of the most beautiful pieces of music every written. The second was one of the great penitential psalms set by Roland de Lassus: "Hear my prayer, O Lord, and let my cry come unto thee / Hide not thy face from me in the day when I am in trouble; incline thine ear unto me" (Ps. 5:1–2). The class was made up of almost all African Americans from the northeast part of the country who had never heard any classical music, much less sacred choral music. Some of them were so overcome they put their heads down on the desk and wept. Nowadays there are about a dozen parishes in this country where this "treasury of sacred music" is regularly sung.

How many times do you hear people come back from Europe, Catholics and non-Catholics alike, and speak glowingly of this cathedral, that organ, or the choir singing chant or polyphony, and how they had never felt so much in the presence of God? Yet we have to suffer through round churches, tabernacles stored away in side chapels, cheerleading cantors, and retreaded Muzak with camp lyrics. One day the beauty of the Church's tradition will be reclaimed, and we will all look back with a hearty laugh.

In Hitchcock's word, there is still much "debris" to be cleared away. I thank God that I met people like Hitchcock, Leiva-Merikakis, and Father Lynch along the way, Catholics who knew where to point an eye hungry for the beauty of God.

✛ *Thirteen* ✛

LEARNING
TO DANCE

M Y READING OF Aquinas and Neo-Thomists, along with the forty pounds of books sent to me by Erasmo, had thoroughly converted my mind to Catholicism. But I knew that was only the beginning.

This was brought home with particular force when I attended my first Mass. I was thoroughly embarrassed by the sitting and standing, disappointed by the bad singing and the worse sermon, and irritated by all the crying babies. I left there knowing I wasn't ready to become Catholic. So I tried other churches: Methodist, Presbyterian, Greek Orthodox, Episcopal. But I could no longer turn back in that direction; I was going to be stuck, for a time, in the in-between. However, these years of bouncing back and forth between Catholic Mass and Protestant worship gave me a much clearer idea of what was at stake in the choice I was about to make. Their respective forms of worship and church governance were as important to the shape of their piety as any theology.

Erasmo once again came to the rescue by introducing me to an Atlanta priest, Father Richard Lopez. Father Lopez and I were both young men then; now he is well known and loved in the diocese of Atlanta. He graciously agreed to meet with me for lunch almost weekly for over a year. He humorously chided me about my largely intellectual and bookish understanding of Catholicism, and he urged me to attend Mass even if I found it hard to follow.

But I continued to be disappointed. I didn't like the sermons or the hymn-singing, if you could even call it singing. The order of Mass printed in the missal was incomprehensible. Everyone else seemed to know what was going on while I flipped the pages furiously; I tried to follow but the order of the service seemed to skip around in the book. I concluded that this was why the missal had several colored ribbons hanging from it. But no one offered to help me. I chuckled, ruminating that if I had been a stranger in a Baptist church not only would I have been led through the service but invited home to lunch as well.

Father Richard Lopez – "Under Father Lopez's guidance I came to see the Catholic Church as the fullest representation of God's revelation to human beings as contained in Scripture."

In all of this confusion there were two things I really liked, and they would keep me coming back to Mass until I started to understand the routine: I liked crossing myself, and I liked kneeling. The motions of the body in Catholic worship helped me to pray and to pay attention in a way I had never done before. I was learning that dance of the Catholic liturgy. It's a series of motions that cradle-Catholics never think about, but as I learned the steps I found them deeply comforting. My body was being enveloped into the faith.

I was also struck by how Catholics left worship in relative silence and waited until they were outside the church before they began to exchange greetings. It was much later that I connected this with the belief in the Real Presence. People tend not to chat idly when they believe that Christ is present a few feet away in the tabernacle.

While I was trying to adjust to these new rituals, Father Lopez was answering my remaining questions regarding the nature of authority, the priesthood, the pope, the Virgin Mary, and the sacraments. The Catholic ban on birth control was something I already affirmed on philosophical grounds, along with the use of natural family planning. I had little difficulty in seeing the superiority of these basic tenets of the Catholic faith given my experience as a Southern Baptist and my growing philosophical appreciation for the tradition of Aristotle and Aquinas. Under Father Lopez's guidance I came to see the Catholic Church as the fullest representation of God's revelation to human beings as contained in Scripture.

The moment of my decision came as a surprise. A close friend of mine, Matt Mancini, with whom I had co-edited a book entitled *Jacques Maritain: Philosopher and Friend,* asked me why I hadn't yet entered the Church. My life had been put on hold by the sudden shattering of a personal relationship, but now I couldn't think of a reason to delay any longer. Later that day I called Father Lopez and asked him to set a date. It's interesting to note that he never pressured me to make a decision; he simply waited for it to happen. I find this is typical of effective Catholic evangelism: there is no need for the hard sell, for the aggressive altar call. You only need to present the Church, point to her truth and beauty. The Church makes her own converts.

When I told Father Lopez I was ready to be confirmed, he told me that he would have to give me an oral exam. I prepared for it by reading Father John Hardon's marvelous *Catholic Catechism*. I am sorry to report that I got a few answers wrong, and I'm not going to reveal which ones.

For my first confession I went back to the monastery at Conyers and met with the monk who had been Erasmo's close friend. Like a good, budding Thomist I structured my confession around the seven deadly sins. My confessor didn't let me get away with the generalities I had prepared. We spent much time talking about my parents and my sisters. I had not realized until then how much baggage I had been carrying around since my Fort Worth days. I had always been told a burden would be lifted in confession, but I wasn't prepared for the demons that were released that day.

For my confirmation Father Lopez chose Our Lady of Perpetual Help Home run by the Hawthorne Dominican Sisters for whom Flannery O'Connor had contributed an introduction to their *Memoir of Mary Ann* published in 1961. I invited a few close friends, including Matt Mancini and his wife, Missy, to the ceremony. The best part of it for me was getting to choose the confirmation name "Thomas."

St. Thomas Aquinas was no longer merely a great teacher; I now bore his name, he was a part of me.

The next morning I went alone to Mass at Immaculate Heart of Mary to receive my first communion. I purposely took no one with me. I was still too close to my Baptist experience and I feared taking too much delight in having others present. It seems silly now. Of course I should have invited those who had taken part in the years of searching. But I wanted to think of nothing but myself before the God I was going to consume for the very first time. I didn't want an audience.

When Father Lopez gave me the Eucharist I forgot to say "Amen." I went back to my seat wondering if after all the preparation I had done it wrong. Maybe my first communion as a Catholic really didn't count? As I sat there worrying about it, I couldn't remember if Father Hardon covered that in his catechism. Father Lopez assured me afterward that everything was all right. I don't think I have forgotten the response since.

Nor have I forgotten my new name. Five years later, only a few days after arriving at Fordham University to teach Thomistic philosophy, I was sideswiped by a car as I drove down the Bronx River

Parkway. I was on the way to a reception for new faculty. The impact knocked me sideways into the guard rail, which I hit at forty-five miles an hour without a seat belt on. As I saw the guard rail approach, in that instant, I said goodbye to my wife and nine-month-old daughter. To my surprise, I was still conscious when my car came to rest in the middle of the parkway. My head was severely cut and bleeding. An off-duty fireman stopped, called an ambulance, and gave me a cloth to press against my scalp while I waited for medical help. Just as I started to lose consciousness I heard the sirens. Hands grabbed me from the driver's seat and placed me on a stretcher. The voices sounded worried. I dimly realized I was in trouble. Then I heard a female voice with a strong Irish brogue scream at me, "You get yourself together, now!" It woke me up, and I found myself suddenly saying the name "Thomas, Thomas." At that moment I became alert and entirely aware of my surroundings inside the EMS vehicle. St. Thomas, I believe, had answered my call for help.

✢ *Fourteen* ✢

NOT AN ANGEL

I WOULD NEVER have made that step into church had it not been for the great intellectual legacy extending from Aristotle through Aquinas to Maritain. Perhaps the most important American-born member of that tradition did not become Catholic until very late in life. But prior to this, his work undoubtedly influenced generations of his readers, including myself, toward the mind of the Church.

Mortimer J. Adler, well known as the godfather of the Great Books movement in the United States, became a Catholic about a year before his death in 2001. I had the great fortune of serving as the first Adler Fellow at the Aspen Institute for three years in the mid-1990s. At the time, he was a practicing and devout Episcopalian after a dramatic conversion in a Chicago hospital bed in 1984.

For years Adler's friends and admirers wondered why he did not become a Catholic. When asked, Adler would say that he had the "will-to-believe, as William James described, but not the gift of faith." After he found himself suddenly repeating the Lord's Prayer in his hospital bed, he asked to be baptized, and his wife, Caroline, brought in an Episcopal priest.

During those summer weeks at Aspen I often talked with Adler about his views on becoming Catholic. He expressed concern about the Church's teaching on abortion and contraception as well as papal authority. I would always respond by reminding him of his own ethics of natural law that led unmistakably to the protection of unborn life and the procreative, as well as the unitive, meaning of the sexual act. At those moments he would throw up his hands and say, "I wish these problems would all go away."

I didn't have the chance to talk to him very much in his final years, so I am not sure what issues finally allowed him to enter the Church he obviously loved since his discovery of Thomas Aquinas as an undergraduate at Columbia University in the 1920s. But I have no doubt from my many conversations with him that it was his own struggle with the problem of angelism that prepared him to enter finally into communion with Rome.

In 1982 Adler published *The Angels and Us.* He argued that whether one cares for the Middle Ages or not, whether one believes in angels or not, there is much to be learned about human nature in meditating on scholastic teaching about the angelic nature of "separated substances."

It can teach us what humans are, and this knowledge enables us to stop infecting our philosophy, ethics, and religion with basic mistakes. These mistakes, I would argue, lend themselves toward a Protestant view of Christianity and get in the way of embracing Catholicism, as Adler eventually did.

What we moderns can discover by contemplating angels, Adler claims, is our failure to grasp the basic unity of human nature, our weakness for an anthropological dualism, and our vulnerability to its consequences. The problems of metaphysical dualism are as old as Plato, who first posited two substances making up the mind and body of human beings. What subsequently became known as angelism is impossible without this Platonic assumption that somehow human intelligence and identity do not depend substantially upon the body. Thus angelism is betrayed by the attitude that human beings are like the pure, immaterial intelligences of the medieval angels, but trapped, temporarily, in their bodies.

It's not uncommon for Christians to believe that in heaven the saved will be transformed into angels. This derives from the assumption that somehow humans are angels in disguise, that our bodies are somehow extraneous to true human nature. Angelism in its most common form is precisely this, an unresolved dualism between the body and the mind. Angelists believe or act as if the material part of ourselves is not really necessary to our nature. The result can be a flight into abstraction, a descent into bestiality, or a zigzagging between the two. In fact, what one sees in Adler's treatment of the history of philosophy is a battle being fought on these two interconnected fronts, on one side against the elevation of human nature toward the angel, and on the other the descent toward the beast.

Angelism began its visit to modernity when some of its key figures — Descartes, in particular — adopted certain features of the medieval teaching on angels to reinforce a sense of individual autonomy. Far from being of quaint historical interest, the results of this appropriation, from Adler's perspective, have

Not an Angel

Mortimer Adler (left) with Deal W. Hudson – "What one sees in Adler's treatment of the history of philosophy is a battle being fought on these two interconnected fronts, on one side against the elevation of human nature toward the angel, and on the other the descent toward the beast."

been enormous — subjectivism and relativism have advanced in epistemology and the philosophy of language, individualism, and hedonism in politics and ethics.

This is not to say that relativism and the rest did not exist before, but that modern angelism offered them fertile ground in which to grow. Legendary and mythic figures like Adam, Faust, and Icarus exemplify the extreme effects of such overreaching, of the unwillingness to accept the limits of the human condition. They form an unhappy chorus with the fallen angel Lucifer himself in cautioning us not to act against the ordinances of nature.

The unity of the material body and immaterial intellect through the form of the soul in human beings is central to the Catholic understanding of philosophy and theology, especially in ethics, politics, epistemology, and education. The loss of that unity, falling either in the direction of the soul *or* the body, is a challenge to the Catholic tradition and apologetics. Think only of the Catholic belief in the real presence of Christ in the Eucharist versus the evangelical understanding of the bread and wine as symbols. For the evangelical at communion the flesh and blood is a name pointing away from itself toward what is not there. For the Catholic there is no need to look away; the eucharistic feast is not understood in nominalist terms, meaning in name only, not in substance. The bread and wine are united with the divine presence analogously to the unity of the mind and body and the divine and human nature in Jesus Christ.

Realizing that as a man I was not an angel in a body was an important step on my road into the Church. I didn't realize that I was prone to this error until I chanced upon Maritain's critique of the

Walker Percy – "The late Walker Percy, a Catholic convert himself, wrote two novels about the struggle with the angel of Dr. Thomas More."

philosopher Descartes in *Three Reformers* and the fictional depictions of angelism in the novels of Walker Percy. When Adler published his book about the same time it felt providential.

The late Walker Percy, a Catholic convert himself, wrote two novels about the struggle with the angel of Dr. Thomas More. More seeks to understand and unify the mind/body rift within himself with drink, women, and, finally, God. *Love in the Ruins* and *The Thanatos Syndrome* follow his trials through different forms of apocalypse in his southern Louisiana parish.

In *Love in the Ruins,* the devil in the character of Art Immelman has stolen an invention from More, a small instrument called a lapsometer, which actually measures the degree of separation of the body from the mind. More thinks that his instrument is "the first caliper of the soul and the first hope of bridging the dread chasm that has rent the soul of Western man ever since the famous philosopher Descartes ripped the body loose from mind and turned the very soul into a ghost that haunts its own house." Immelman wants to use the lapsometer to widen, rather than close, the gap, making men feel godlike and happy.

In both novels, More struggles to overcome his own self-division while trying to defeat those who would exacerbate this condition. In the sequel, *The Thanatos Syndrome,* a group of eugenicists actually takes up this project on a mass scale and starts adding heavy sodium to the water supply. Unlike Immelman, who knows the falseness of his promises, the doctors think a happy society will result from the elimination of psychological suffering. The sodium treatments result in a brutal sex scene between adults and children that startled Percy's readers and still troubles some of them today.

Percy wanted to make the message unmistakable: avoid the pain and suffering of a human life, one constituted by the unity of body and soul, and you risk loosing demons. The very complacency and ersatz happiness produced by disjunction between the mind and body becomes the occasion of the cruel elimination of the unwanted and the imperfect, including children, the handicapped, and the infirm.

At the novel's end, Father Smith preaches what has to be the most powerful homily in modern literature; at its apex he repeats twice the following thought: " 'Don't you know where tenderness leads?' Silence. 'To the gas chambers.' " Percy's Father Smith is echoing a comment previously made by Flannery O'Connor in her introduction to *A Memoir of Mary Ann:* "In the absence of faith, we govern by tenderness, and tenderness leads to the gas chamber." Acts of tenderness that extinguish life to eliminate suffering are cruel; they are based on the conclusion that a life isn't worth living if the pain of the body destroys self-satisfaction. Such acts reject not only faith in the goodness of creation but also the unity of the human person. This is not to say that suffering should be regarded as good in itself, but to acknowledge a necessity of finitude and bodily existence. Since they are detached from reality, dualists always pay a price: those devoted to bestialism darken their minds by ignoring them, while angelists run from pain into false utopias where nonexistence is forced upon those whose sufferings disqualify them for life.

Like Maritain and Adler, Percy traced this condition back to the influence of Descartes and his use of methodical doubt in the pursuit of certainty. In his *Meditations,* Descartes systematically disregarded the testimony of his senses and his passions in order to discover a secure basis for knowledge. The only way Descartes could find a basis of certainty once he abandoned the senses was in the inherent clarity of ideas as guaranteed by the truthfulness of God. In other words, human beings know like the angels of medieval philosophy that Descartes studied; we know by the direct illumination of God.

The Catholic tradition as witnessed in Adler, Maritain, and Percy has always insisted that human beings are a unity of body and mind. The soul itself is the form that unites the material and immaterial parts of the human person. This is why the Church teaches that when the individual is resurrected, a spiritual body enters into heaven, insuring that the integrity of the human person is placed before God, not some angelic version of the individual who lived on earth.

The impulse to angelism can be seen wherever there is a fear of the body and impatience with mysterious matters. Angelism in religion is still represented in American culture by vestiges of Puritanism, with its repression of the body, its abstract certainty of a religious calling, and its separation from sinful society.

But nothing trumps angelism like the Incarnation. The scandal of the Word becoming flesh, of divine and human nature joined into one person, reiterates God's love for the nature he created when he made Adam and Eve. The angelist who is unwilling to admit the mind's dependence upon the sense will find the union of divine and human natures in Christ unthinkable, much less the Church as the Body of Christ in history.

✤ *Fifteen* ✤

BEAUTY AND CONVERSION

THE IDEA OF CONVERSION and the idea of beauty seem to exist on different levels of moral seriousness, at least in the minds of some. To those people, the experience of the beautiful seems too subjective or too dangerous to carry redemptive significance.

Catholic intellectuals of the first rank, such as Father William F. Lynch, Jacques Maritain, and Hans Urs von Balthasar, have labored to keep beauty from being dismissed by successive generations of Catholic faithful. Like our evangelical brethren, devoted Catholics are continually tempted toward an abstract rationalism — stripped of aesthetic interest — in defense of a much-battered faith.

Rationalism treats truth without concern for either the role of sense or the necessity of personal appropriation. Rationalism denotes an approach to truth that recognizes only mental activity as a way of receiving and affirming the truths of human existence.

Rationalism, in short, forgets the body. It asserts the primacy of self-conscious inference over the spontaneous, intuitive reception of luminous presence. It recognizes argument and ignores vision.

To be sure, there are good reasons for rationalism. Intuitive vision and aesthetic experience in general do not stand the test of public verification in any scientific sense. This does not mean, however, that they cannot be part of a philosophical or theological understanding of how persons convert to a new and different understanding of life and its proper end. But rationalism would, if it could, limit philosophical and theological discourse solely to that which is verifiable.

The genius of the philosopher Maritain and theologians von Balthasar and Lynch is that they hung on tightly to human experience. As Maritain once remarked, Thomists need "soft bodies" in order to be receptive to experience that speaks of God. They clung to what subjects experience in their lifelong journey toward God. Human subjects don't just live in bodies. They are bodies.

What does this obvious fact imply? It implies the centrality, and the unavoidability, of the *aesthetic*, derived from the Greek *aesthesis*, meaning sense experience. But once again, we confront a pervasive problem of expectations. To speak of aesthetics, for most people, is to address matters of high culture. This is a fundamental error. The aesthetic, in its foundational sense, is the doorway to all knowledge and the acquisition of all value.

The reason why a convert need not be ashamed of touting beauty as his entryway into the faith is because we must begin with the body. Indeed, I am surprised by conversion stories that consist only of intellectual arguments and closely rendered interpretations of various texts, whether scriptural or theological. It is my understanding of human love that persons require some stimulus exciting the will to act.

Something must initially be seen in order for such intellectual exercises even to begin. What causes desire, what motivates the will, is the "sight" of something beautiful or something good. This is the classic relationship between the will and the intellect, the former being the running power and the latter the catching power.

Since we are not angels and do not receive the direct illumination of nature, we would be completely cut off from the world and ourselves without the senses. We would never love, much less think. Von Balthasar said in the first volume of *The Glory of the Lord* that "whoever sneers at her [beauty's] name as if she were the ornament of a bourgeois past — whether he admits it or not — can no longer pray and soon will no longer be able to love."

It was certainly true in my own case that these many encounters led to my ultimate conversion. All the hundreds of books that I read, the hours of music that I heard, the conversations, the arguments, the disputes, the friends lost and gained, the years of uncertainty and doubt, all were grounded in particular moments of inarticulate vision.

In the experience of beauty, there are three elements present. Most casual conversations about beauty fail to distinguish between them and confusion usually results. First there is the object of beauty itself; then there is the subject, or the viewer, who sensually perceives beauty; and finally there is the relationship that is created between object and subject.

The subject of aesthetic experience can be further subdivided into those who create objects of art and those who experience them.

Most of what I can say about beauty and my conversion is confined to my experience of it, but I don't believe that this relegates me to a pure subjectivism. In the experience of beauty, we are responding to the perception of form in objects or actions. That form is attractive to the human mind because it displays order and clarity in the midst of complexity. In beauty, mind glimpses the handiwork of mind. Or as Dorothy Sayers would put it, we observe "the mind of the Maker."

The ecstatic experience that is at the heart of seeing the beautiful — that delicious moment of going outside oneself — is a response to the ecstasy of creation, whether creation by the human or divine artist. The creator moves outside himself by making an object conform to an inner vision or intuition. Thus, beauty is made possible by intelligence, both in the subject who sees it and in the artist who makes what we delight in.

It is often said in the tradition of St. Thomas and the Neoplatonists that beauty is one of the transcendental attributes of being itself. Beauty as a transcendental is never perceived directly, any more than any other transcendental can be known imme-diately. However, the experience of finite beauty is undoubtedly grounded in the transcendent beauty that belongs to all being. Transcendent beauty, like transcendent goodness, persists regardless of the destructive forces of ugliness or evil.

Just as Satan himself retains the goodness of his being, as St. Thomas teaches, he also retains the beauty of his existence. To be trumps *not* to be.

This explains why beauty has the power to convert. To say this may belabor the obvious to most people. We all know that beauty is used to sell any and all products. We all know that personal beauty is one of the greatest advantages in life, in spite of its appar-ent disadvantages. We all know that beauty gets our attention, keeps it, and lifts our spirits and distracts us from the boredom of everyday life. So to ask why beauty converts is to raise a question that really lies at the heart of our everyday experience. We all can agree that beauty attracts our attention because beauty, by definition, is that which delights the senses.

This, in fact, is the classic definition of beauty given by St. Thomas Aquinas. Being delightful, beauty im-mediately becomes the object of appetite and will; that is, beauty appears to us as desirable under the form of the good. Herein, of course, lies the danger of beauty. Its experience leads us out toward the possibility of embracing some new, perhaps destructive, object of love.

Let it be said quite clearly that not all conversions are for the good, that beauty does not necessarily serve the angels. The moral meaning of beauty is intrinsically ambiguous: which is to say, beauty can lead us to heaven or to hell. I think that, despite this ambiguity, there is a strong impulse within the experience of beauty itself that is in line with Plato's teaching in the *Symposium:* Any experience of beauty opens a wound that can be healed only by contact with a greater beauty, a greater good. In other words, aesthetic experience can be, from a moral perspective, self-correcting.

This is not an argument I am prepared to develop or even defend at length here. But I do think that the understanding of beauty as proposed by Aquinas and later Thomists puts the person who develops a genuine critical appreciation for the beautiful at an advantage in the search for ultimate reality. When Satan uses beauty to seduce us away from God, he is using that which belongs to God. He is disordering that which is fundamentally ordered to the Creator.

To summarize, beauty converts us because it attracts, it elicits desire, and it makes us yearn for unity with itself. Beauty converts us because in unifying ourselves with it, we become new. This is why we always must take care in what we choose to love, or perhaps better to say what we are moved to love, because what we love will change us over time.

Given my perspective, you will understand if I say bad taste is no little matter. Bad taste leads to a union — through affectivity — with things that can diminish us. Bad taste, in fact, is a habit of clinging to what may defile, demean, and diminish us. Our entertainments, in short, are not trivial pursuits.

In telling this story of beauty and conversion, I don't want to leave you with the impression that I, Deal Hudson, convert to the Catholic faith, once twenty years ago underwent a series of extraordinary experiences that led me to convert.

I would rather leave you with the impression that I have been blessed with a constant experience of conversion, one that began in a dramatic way, worthy perhaps of public telling. But if any of us, whether converts or not, ever stop converting, then we have all fallen short of the vision we originally received.

Sixteen

BEAUTY WILL SAVE THE WORLD

ONE OF THE CHARACTERS in Dostoevsky's novel *The Idiot* says, "Beauty will save the world." That was clever of Dostoevsky: By saying it through one of his characters he doesn't have to defend it.

I'm going out on a limb to say precisely that: beauty will save the world. And I will have to defend against those who find it objectionable.

But how do you defend a proposition that is not, strictly speaking, demonstrable?

I must admit that my certainty in this matter is grounded in experience, my own and that of many others who have found the lure of beauty irresistible. Thus the defense of beauty does not consist of an aesthetic; it requires telling stories, one after another, of beauty's saving effect. To this the skeptic will declare,

"You believe that beauty will save the world because you were saved by beauty."

Of course what I believe about my own experience does not prove anything in itself. And, to make matters worse, even though it's my experience I cannot be sure in telling my story that I am telling the entire truth. We have no privileged access to knowing ourselves; the soul, as Aquinas says, cannot look at itself.

What may make my story convincing to others is that others may recognize themselves in it. Or they may recognize something they aspire to. The story may help in the daunting task of self-knowledge.

I have found that the lure of beauty, so to speak, has been the pivot point for many conversion stories of all kinds across many ages.

So what I offer here is neither a metaphysics of beauty nor a theological aesthetics. This is a story of my unexpected, and unsought, encounters with beautiful things that ultimately led me beyond them.

The lure of beauty has been recognized in the Christian tradition again and again. For me it was Jacques Maritain who first opened my eyes to it, but it is the comprehensive work of the late Hans Urs von Balthasar whose majestic *The Glory of the Lord* has made theological reflection on aesthetics finally acceptable.

But these exercises, as the reader will see, are not uniform, they do not unfold systematically or even chronologically. My conversion cannot be summarized as a reading of texts or encounters with music and poetry. My life, I hope, doesn't consist of a series of reviews.

In Plato's *Symposium*, Socrates presents the view that experience of finite beauty creates a continual hunger for infinite beauty — the beauty of the body leads to the beauty of the soul and onward to the Beautiful itself. If conversions always resulted accordingly one would be led from, say, Bach's *B Minor Mass* toward the God who is praised in the composer's music. But the effect of beauty on the restless soul is often not that straightforward. For example, many will recall that beauty played an important role in Augustine's conversion. Augustine became conscience-stricken when he realized that his emotional reaction to suffering on a stage was greater than his response to the same suffering in real life. This led him to examine his dependence on sensual enjoyment and look within for the immaterial traces of God's presence.

Whereas Augustine's soul was pricked by his emotional reaction to works of the imagination, as opposed to the world he lived in, mine was stirred by guilt about being drawn to the world of beauty at all, a world deeply distrusted in my evangelical surroundings.

The religious leaders I knew would have regarded Dostoevsky's statement "beauty will save the world" as trite at best and at worst superficial and morally irresponsible. These moralists regard beauty only as an occasion of sensual sin, a temptation to disregard the true things of the spirit.

Part of the story I have to tell is how I overcame what I felt was a religious prohibition against beauty, a prohibition that I found antithetical to the full glory of God's grace. In this I was aided most of all by the Catholic novel. To the religious reader wary of the aesthetic, the novel has the advantage of being content-rich about human life. Reading a Catholic novel, you are reading about God and humankind, heaven and hell, sin and forgiveness: you can be assured that the act of reading is not the wasteful effort of a "carnal mind."

✢ Seventeen ✢

CATHOLIC
NOVELS

Reading, said St. Josémaría Escrivá, has made many a saint. In my own case it has merely made a convert, but I do continue to read ever more deeply into the mystery that is the Church. Thomas Merton started on his road to the Church with the accidental discovery of Etienne Gilson's *The Spirit of Medieval Philosophy* in the Columbia University Library. We are foolish to forget the power of the written word.

As I moved toward the Church, my reading prodded me onward with a series of vaguely related insights. Although I understood only a little of the content of the Catholic faith, I knew that it explained the limitations of the Christian traditions, both liberal Protestant and Southern Baptist, in which I was raised. It would take me years to pass through my own period of protest and grasp the inner coherence of the Church herself. I was a young college professor then, and still reeling from the effect of the Catholic bomb, when I began to read Catholic novels, one after another. By the time I finished this assignment — luckily I had wise and tasteful tutors — I would not have dreamed of turning back.

There are, in fact, Catholic novels, though certain learned people dispute the fact. I have no comprehensive definition of the Catholic novel, neither would I ever attempt one. However, I happily name a novel as Catholic when it presents to the reader a narrative that embodies some substantial aspect of the Catholic faith. In other words, a Catholic novel is one that ably suggests to its reader moments of insight, where we catch a glimpse of God's ineluctable providence — as in, for example, *Diary of a Country Priest* — so that readers become pilgrims.

It is said that people don't read much anymore, that we live in a multimedia age, and that the act of reading is on the wane. I don't take these prognostications too seriously. Nothing is likely to replace reading as the most intimate medium of enjoyment and self-examination — certainly not a CD-ROM or the Web. When we want to change a person's life, we still give that person a book, and wait, hoping.

As you've seen, I had been raised in a Protestant home and had become an ardent Southern Baptist in college before attending Princeton Theological Seminary. There I read the greats — Luther, Calvin, Barth, Tillich, and the Niebuhrs. I began to realize that the first principle of Protestantism — ridding the faith of idolatry — had gone so far as to undermine Christian intelligence. My Catholic bomb was packed with many spiritual and theological books, from the great Dominican Garrigou-Lagrange and Maisie Ward on G. K. Chesterton, to the simple verse of St. Francis of Assisi. With every book, a strong impression received years earlier when I had read St. Augustine's *On the Trinity* was confirmed: Catholic Christianity embodied the fullness of God's revelation, without the narrowing refractions of other, younger Christian communions.

The first principle of Catholicism was indeed the Incarnation, and that centrality shone through all my reading. Thus, if there is a litmus test for the Catholic novel, it must be whether the novel is capable of conspiring in spiritual conversion. Even if one bears in mind that conversion is ongoing, not at all confined to a Damascus Road experience, this test flies in the face of most aesthetic niceties about the freedom of the writer, the novel, and the audience. It goes without saying that authors who consciously intend to convert their readers probably will end up doing a poor job. That's the trouble with avid readers, like myself, giving in to speculations: we risk encouraging the worst habits of young novelists. Among the novels that led me to the Church, I want to recommend the following:

Brideshead Revisited by Evelyn Waugh

If there is another novel that wears its moral consciousness as lightly as Evelyn Waugh's *Brideshead Revisited,* I don't know it. Perhaps that is why it works so well. Like Charles Ryder himself, the reader is slowly and slyly seduced into the Catholic undercurrents of the aristocratic Marchmain family. The long, final coda of Lord Marchmain's death, his sign of the cross, and the repentant confession of Julia on the staircase distill the choice we all must finally make *for* or *against* God. As Julia puts it, in refusing to leave her husband for Charles, "But I saw today there was one thing unforgivable . . . the bad thing I was on the point of doing, that I'm not quite bad enough to do; to set up a rival good to God's."

The Other One by Julian Green

The still-active French-American writer Julian Green, born of a Protestant mother from Savannah, Georgia, and a French Catholic father, has riveted my attention for years. Although his novels, like *Moira* and *Each in His Own Darkness,* are better known, it was the obscure *The Other One* that left its deepest mark on me. This novel, more than any other I know, depicts the hunger for God as the source of all human appetites. I would later recognize this unquenchable desire, with its rich moral implications, in Aquinas's anthropology — but I first met it in Green. Set in Copenhagen, the story follows a recently converted man who returns to a woman he had mistreated some years earlier only to find the results of his immorality much worse than expected. His penitential witness brings about a disturbing but absolutely convincing redemption. Few books have captured the painful death of spiritual rebirth, in both characters, as powerfully as *The Other One.*

Kristin Lavransdatter by Sigrid Undset

I'm not sure if there is a greater Catholic novel than this one; if there is, it's probably her other medieval epic, *The Master of Hestviken*, but I still prefer the more accessible *Kristin*.

The first time I read Undset's trilogy, I was blessed with a very bad case of the flu, which kept me in bed for the entire read. My bouts with fever only intensified my connection with the unforgettable characters of the story. Just as movie buffs will argue the comparative merits of Scarlet, Rhett, Melanie, and Ashley in *Gone with the Wind*, so Undset fans delight in assigning degrees of responsibility to the impetuous Kristin, her loyal father, Lavrans, her warrior husband, Erlend, and her jilted fiancé, the foursquare Simon. No other novel that I know explores the biblical themes of the "the wages of sin" and "the sins of the father" as accurately and charitably as *Kristin Lavransdatter*. Its impact on the reader, as witnessed in the novel's pivotal role in the life of Dorothy Day, founder of the Catholic Worker movement, can demonstrate a moral reorientation reminiscent of Dante's *Purgatorio*. I was able to pay a spiritual debt to Undset by editing a book, *Sigrid Undset on Saints and*

Sigrid Undset – "No other novel that I know explores the biblical themes of the 'the wages of sin' and 'the sins of the father' as accurately and charitably as *Kristin Lavransdatter.*"

Sinners, containing previously untranslated writing and critical essays.

Love in the Ruins by Walker Percy

My reading into the Church was not without its moments of laughter. This novel provided the perfect bridge from the existentialism of my graduate school days to the treasure of Catholic humanism. I thought it uncanny that Percy had placed his main character, Dr. Thomas More, in a Dantean landscape faced with Kierkegaardian choices that could be mediated only by the comic, sacramental resolution of a Catholic vision. It was as if Percy — and his other novels confirm this — had already experienced my philosophical and spiritual trials; he understood that demons inhabited the suburbs of my childhood, and not just the cities and the country.

Wise Blood by Flannery O'Connor

If you are familiar with the South, there is also plenty to laugh about in Flannery O'Connor's *Wise Blood.* John Huston's underrated film of the novel catches many of those moments perfectly, such as when

Hazel Motes tells his landlady he is a preacher of the "Church without Christ." She asks suspiciously, was that "Protestant...or something foreign?" Indeed, O'Connor's novel is nothing less than a meditation on the loss of belief in Christ's active presence in the world through the Church and its sacraments. *Wise Blood* made it clear to me why I was no longer content with the typical Protestant quarterly communion of grape juice done "*in memory* of me."

Under the Star of Satan by Georges Bernanos

If O'Connor is one of those authors who puts you in the uncomfortable presence of the supernatural, Georges Bernanos is another. It's too bad that *Diary of a Country Priest* is his only novel that stays in print, because the others are just as powerful. *Under the Star of Satan* is primarily about the special vocation of the priesthood, and its sacramental blessing on all of us. We follow the protagonist, Abbé Donissan, modeled on Jean-Marie Vianney, the Curé of Ars, as he struggles for the soul of his parishioners, spending hour after hour in the confessional. We see his gift of unlocking the heaviest heart and the price he must pay for it. In the midst of Donissan's battle, we are also reminded not to take the metaphysical notion of evil as privation so literally as to discount its active presence in the world. A film has been made of this novel, but not as successfully as *Wise Blood*. Robert Bresson's film *The Diary of a Country Priest* ranks as one of the most spiritually compelling films ever made.

These are six of the novels that made me Catholic. There are many others from our rich cultural past I could recommend, especially homegrown Catholic writers like J. F. Powers, Edwin O'Connor, and Jon Hassler. The Canadian writer Morley Callahan, a friend and sparring partner of Ernest Hemingway, deserves a revival. The fiction of the English writer Muriel Spark grows in stature as time passes. In fact, we are witnessing a modest revival of good Catholic fiction — Alice Thomas Ellis, Torgny Lindgren, Ron Hansen, Piers Paul Read, and Ralph McInerny are among the best. We can only pray that books such as theirs will be found upon the path of some pilgrim finding a way home.

✢ *Eighteen* ✢

CONTRASTING AESTHETICS

A T THE TIME OF MY CONVERSION, I was accused by various friends of converting for aesthetic reasons. Even if I harbored such motives, the more Masses I went to, the more I realized they didn't measure up to the midnight Masses televised from the Vatican. In fact, liturgical practice was so bad — lousy music, weak homilies, half-hearted gestures — I came to see a definite irony in the experience of beauty that helped lure me into the Church. At least in the liturgies I was attending, with the exception of St. Ignatius Loyola in New York City, where my family attended for several years, the Masses seemed more dispirited than what I had expected.

Yes, I first learned to love Catholicism from books and would inevitably be disappointed by actual participation in the day-to-day life of the Church. Expectations raised by the glories of Dante, Aquinas, Newman, and Maritain are soon disappointed by contemporary parish architecture, sloppiness in liturgical execution, inattentive congregations, the lack of fellowship (compared to evangelicals), and, most important, the increasing approximation of Protestant worship and piety in many Catholic parishes.

In recent years there have been various attempts to revitalize the sense of community in Catholic parishes. These programs sometimes turn the sanctuary into a fellowship hall in the manner of evangelicals, forgetting the reverence owed the Presence in the tabernacle (unless, of course, He has been placed elsewhere!). Catholics must learn to meet and greet people naturally, without imitating an evangelical style that does not integrate into Catholic liturgy. Evangelicals have been throwing parties in their churches for decades; Catholics don't have a clue how to do it, and should stop trying.

The older generation of Catholics were used to attending Mass quietly, without much participation. There were other opportunities in these older, more tightly knit communities to create and enjoy friendship, such as at the parish school. Where these institutions no longer exist, the younger generations are understandably finding it difficult to engender the warmth of fellowship that they can find at the Baptist church across the street.

These concerns bother me less now since they betray a Protestant penchant for making the reality of worship, and church life in general, dependent on the enthusiasm and skillful execution of the preacher or congregation. If I understand the meaning of the Mass, its reality is in no way dependent upon the skill or charisma of the celebrant, although it may benefit from both in its aesthetic power to claim our attention.

Perhaps I was having trouble getting used to the repetition of the Catholic Mass, which is basically the same from week to week during ordinary time. Kierkegaard, after all, had warned me against the impossibility of "aesthetic repetition," meaning that repetition of the same experience rarely produces the pleasure it induces the first time. Baptist and all evangelically tinged Protestant churches avoid the problem of aesthetic repetition with the personality and charisma of the minister. A powerful homily always leads to Sunday afternoon dinner conversation devoted to evaluating the performance of the pastor — the success of worship depending upon his eloquence. The Protestant pastor bears a heavy burden to be original, creative, and innovative. The Catholic priest depends only on the sacramental nature of the eucharistic act; he does not have a stage to compete with MTV, the way megachurches now have with projection screens, lights, and high power audio. The priest simply repeats the ancient words.

Protestant worship seems to be much more preoccupied with the aesthetics of the personalities and charisms while the Mass, although enjoying aesthetic form, remains exactly the same regardless of time, place, or person. Thus, the reality of Jesus Christ remains the same for us at all times, regardless of our transient feelings or our capacity for attention. Protestant worship with its entire focus on the preaching of the Word unwittingly promotes the cult of the pastor's personality (or brilliance), which explains why Protestant churches rise and fall with the coming and going of the minister. What a burden for the Protestant pastor to bear without the objectivity of the eucharistic act to celebrate! This probably explains why their sermons are so articulate. They have to be. Of course, these criticisms of Protestant worship are aimed at the deeper level of the articulated and un-articulated Baptist credo: the Protestant suspicion of embodiment — especially into space — of the Holy and its all too pessimistic fear of idols.

For Protestants, the word in time is trusted, the spoken word, as if it were more living for its momentary duration, like that passing wind of the Holy Spirit. This orientation toward inspired and charismatic personality is synonymous with the direction of modern life and the influence of the media on our standards of judgment. Often the Catholic Church and its worship will seem "medieval" or "uninteresting" by comparison; for me it has taken some getting used to. There are times I miss the full-throated hymn-singing of a Baptist congregation, especially on Easter morning. My wife had to grab my sleeve once in a suburban New York parish on Easter when I was so upset that no one was singing "Jesus Christ Is Risen Today" that I was going to walk into the aisle and say so!

The Mass is a ritual in time of sanity and calm, where no one should expect to be entertained, and no one should mistake the adrenalin of religious enthusiasm for creedal certainty. The worst thing the Catholic Church could do is to give the Mass away to those who want to "jazz it up" by stealing our silence. At least a lackluster liturgy keeps us from the heresy of emotivism, that is, identifying our feeling states with our beliefs.

It is the liturgical celebration of the Eucharist that ensures avoidance of aesthetic dialectics: "making things interesting or relevant." Catholic liturgy resists the encroachment of enthusiasms and charisms that come and go claiming to make everything alive, real, authentic, true again. The Mass is freedom from the cult of feeling — the equation of truth with the intensity of sensation or heightened self-awareness.

The same problems that I find at the heart of Protestant worship I also find in its theology, piety, and ecclesiology: each of the problems is in the same way associated with a resurgent subjectivity, a misplaced trust in the inspired individual, whether pastor or layman. Theologically, this is seen as the Protestant "priesthood of the believer" with its implicit promotion of anyone's inspired relationship to the Bible. In this piety and spiritual formation one finds inspired individuals who are free to proclaim that God told them to do such and such, and no one has the authority to say otherwise and deny it. The effect of this constant "underground" of enthusiasm, as Catholic historian Frederich Heer calls it in his unparalleled *Intellectual History of Europe*, plays havoc in the life of the Church, eventually emerging as the Protestant movement led by the monk Martin Luther. The lack of theological authority, other than personal readings of the Scriptures, naturally leads to myriad inter-pretations, each spawning its own church, which is inevitably doomed by its own substructure to spawn a few more.

Of course, the typical response to all of this is a series of questions concerning the nature and le-gitimacy of the Catholic hierarchical authority. The major flaw in these questions is that they fail from the beginning to see these institutions as gifts to us, gifts that we need for life on earth, for spiritual growth. Instead they are seen as unnecessary impediments to our freedom, as if mere potentiality were valuable in itself. And even worse, it is as if the very means af-forded to us by God for our peace and joy were being rejected so that we can do it for ourselves, and be more authentic and less childish. I am speaking here of the authority of the sacraments, the priest, and the power of the magisterium and pope. Occam's razor does not apply to things of the spirit that have come as gifts, not as logical necessities.

Nonetheless even these things of the spirit are ratified by common sense. One can see this especially concerning confession. How many therapists would be put out of business if we took advantage of this great opportunity? The priests, the confessional, the Eucharist, the pope himself, are all gifts to us in the same way that prayer is. And indeed, the same argument is made against prayer in favor of "meditation," the latter being a way of "getting in touch with yourself" without having to look toward some transcendent Being when it is actually your own being you are concerned about.

The principle of the Incarnation is at stake in all of this: whether we believe that God has become flesh to be among us. Protestants allow God his historical presence in his Church, his Body — a concept that has more than biblical warrant to satisfy the most ardent skeptic. The Church is the Body of Christ; this perhaps sums up what I have found in Catholicism that I did not find in Protestantism. The Protestant insistence on inspired enthusiasm and charism rather than on revealed, deposited doctrine, on Scriptures apart from their interpretation by the Church in history, denies the actual, real presence of Christ in the Church.

✢ *Nineteen* ✢

JULIAN GREEN

J ULIAN GREEN is well known in France but familiar to very few in the United States. Green was born in 1900 to an American mother from Savannah, Mary Hartridge Green, and a French father. His bond with his southern Calvinist mother, whose father was a Confederate officer, was extremely close, though she died when he was only fourteen. In spite of becoming perhaps the most cosmopolitan writer in a cosmopolitan city — Paris — he kept a large Confederate flag on the wall of his apartment on the rue de Vaneau. He once described himself as "a Southerner lost in Europe, regardless of what I do."

Green published eighteen novels before he died in 1998. His many volumes of journals made his private life one of the most public in France and constitute a cultural history of Paris, with the exception of his sojourn at the University of Virginia from 1919 to 1922, and the war years, 1940 to 1945, which he spent around Washington, D.C. In 1971 he became the first writer with American citizenship to be admitted to the Academie Française, taking the place of Catholic author François Mauriac, whom Green eulogized upon his entry.

Green converted to Catholicism soon after the death of his mother, but over the course of his long life his chosen faith would constantly be struggling against his own sexual tendencies toward other men. He was outside of the Church for twenty years (1919–39) and though he never lost faith, he could not pray.

Of all the novelists I read on my way into the Church none touched me more deeply than Julian Green. I am ashamed to admit that I had to rely on translations of his, I am told, very beautiful French. But thanks to artful translators, including his sister Ann Green, I was introduced to a fictional landscape of faith and sexuality that allowed me, for the first time, to comprehend erotic desire in the context of divine creation.

A passage from his diaries reads: "What I have against a life of pleasure is that it kills in a man all

Julian Green – "Of all the novelists I read on my way into the Church none touched me more deeply than Julian Green."

aptitude for love. It gives him the heart of a eunuch. I said this to someone who was piqued by my remarks, but I feel strongly that I am right. Nothing is colder than a pleasure-loving man. This is perceptible only in the long run, because during youth there exists the eternal misunderstanding about desire and love, which are taken one for the other. Love is not necessarily linked to desire; it surpasses it continually, but love is not to be met every day, it does not run about the streets: in fact, that is precisely what it never does" (March 3, 1955).

Love surpasses desire because, as Green helped to show me, love is finally directed at God. Most of his novels reflect this struggle between sexual desire and the desire for God, a battle that often leads his characters toward violence or suicide. The source of Green's scrutiny of this subject is surely his mother's Puritanism, so graphically described in his journals and memoirs. It's hard to forget the scene he describes of waking up one morning as an adolescent with his first erection and going to his mother to ask her what was wrong. She proceeded to grab a knife from the kitchen and chase poor Julian around the house trying to cut it off. That kind of episode would haunt most of our imaginations for years to come!

Though it's easy to recognize the author's pre-occupations in the actions of his characters, his novels are in no way written to express a Catholic message. Green the Catholic writer remains artfully hidden, and his characters, which Green once said he "prayed for," are substantially drawn and memorable.

I read all of the novels available in translation, including *Moira* (1950), *Each in His Own Darkness* (1960), and *The Trangressor* (1955), but it was and still is *The Other One* (1971) that held the greatest meaning for me. Here Green treats the story of Roger, who returns to the scene of his seduction of a young woman named Karin to seek her forgiveness. But finding that her life has been filled with a series of degradations, including a loss of faith, during the German occupation of Denmark, Roger feels responsible for her ruin.

Green's narration looks at the seduction and its aftermath from the differing points of view of the seducer and the seduced: the seduction itself is told by Roger, while Karin relates Roger's return ten years later to receive forgiveness. Roger's seduction of the innocent Karin is deliberately destructive not only of her virginity but also of her faith. Karin, who knows she is being used, is helpless to avoid him. What taints his seduction, however, is not the bore-dom that follows sexual conquest but his knowledge that she gave in to his aggression knowingly. Roger wanted his desire to overwhelm his prey, but Karin's choice to leave the Church and sleep with Roger mitigates his satisfaction.

Years later when Roger returns to find the now "ruined" Karin, she muses on the difference between sexual desire in men and women:

"Deep down my sensuality was no more than a thirst for affection. It was this that had been quenched in physical frenzy. With that annihilating joy would I have folded my arms, which now held no one, round a being I could cherish! There was something in me that refused to make of a man an instrument of sexual pleasure. My soul demanded much more than that. Surely every woman would understand me. Is it our fault if their constant pangs of bodily hunger throw men into a state nearing mad-ness? Because it is with half-mad people that we have to deal. If they could only see themselves at cer-tain moments.... As for women, they never entirely lose their heads and can only observe the appalling misunderstanding when they see lust trying to pass itself off as love. On this point they cannot explain themselves, since men use the same words as they do, but to indicate things of a different nature. Women love and men love, but only their bodies are united. There are sublime exceptions, I know, such as are treated in poetry. I am not denying that these unique moments occur, but speaking generally, for a man variety is the rule and the bed is the tomb of love, or rather of one love after another. With that self-sufficiency does the king of creation bestow a plural on this word where he himself is concerned! His precious loves . . . and the fact that he can't count them makes him think that he's a great lover, whereas in his headlong rush he misses out on love in the singular."

Few writers treat the relation of sex to salvation and sanctity as deftly as Green. Sexual yearning did not belong to some netherworld of physical needs but for the desire for God itself. Thus Green's fiction fleshes out the oft-quoted "restless heart" of St. Augustine. Some religious readers would rather read about restless hearts in the abstract than be exposed to the sinners of Green's fiction. These readers who tend to view all art through a moral prism before allowing themselves to enjoy it consider stories like that of Roger and Karin an occasion of sin rather than an occasion of spiritual insight. Their reticence puts them in a difficult situation regarding the Catholic novel, since so much important Catholic fiction revolves around an incident of adultery or seduction — *Brideshead Revisited, Kristin Lavransdatter, Wise Blood, The End of the Affair,* to name a few.

Green himself, with his own Puritan upbringing, was alive to the irony:

"Drag a writer away from his sin and he no longer writes. This, I admit, is a horrible statement to put into words. Is sin necessary to his works? Who would dare say such a thing? But remove sin and you remove the works. Are the works necessary? You might as well ask if a writer is necessary. He is inasmuch as God wishes him to exist. . . . I can withdraw from the world, as I have so often been tempted to do, but then, no more works. Now, I believe that I came into this world to write books and to reach a few people" (May 3, 1954).

The greatest of Catholic poets, Dante, was also aware that his readers might raise the question, so he answered them at the beginning of his *Divine Comedy:*

Midway the path of life that men pursue
I found me in a darkling wood astray,
For the direct way had been lost to view.
Ah me, how hard a thing it is to say
What was this thorny wildwood intricate
Whose memory renews the first dismay!
Scarcely in death is bitterness more great:
But as concerns the good discovered there
The other things I saw will I relate.

(Musa translation)

These "other things" are what make so many morally earnest religious readers cringe when reading fiction or viewing theater, film, painting, or sculpture. But it's clear from the history of Christian art that Green is absolutely correct: avoid the sin and you kill the creative imagination of the artist. The artist has been deprived of the material cause of his creation.

The Catholic tradition, to its credit, has always recognized this and thus many artists have found a home there. Puritanism in any guise, even when it quotes St. Thomas Aquinas, kills the imagination and strips truth of its sensuous splendor.

✠ Twenty ✠

MEETING
MARITAIN

B Y THE TIME I discovered Jacques Maritain in
1980, his star had been in decline for a decade or more. The onetime leader of the French and
American Catholic Renascence was being accused
of turning reactionary in his old age. His *Peasant of
the Garonne,* with its criticism of Teilhard de Chardin,
phenomenology, and the abuses following Vatican II,
made him a pariah among those luxuriating in the
mood of change pervading the Church and culture
of the late 1960s.

The occasion of my meeting with Maritain was
the 1980 American Catholic Philosophical Association meeting in St. Louis. I had ventured there on
a whim, thinking that with my newfound love of

St. Thomas and things Catholic I would surely meet kindred spirits, and fortunately I was correct.

In the back pages of the program I saw that an organization called the American Maritain Association was having a meeting on "Art and Beauty," and that the featured speakers would be discussing his books *Art and Scholasticism* and *Creative Intuition in Art and Poetry*. Warmly met by the association's treasurer and his wife, Tony and Judy Simon, and enthralled by a group of Catholic philosophers devoted to the subject of beauty, I was hooked instantly. For the next fourteen years of my life I sought to build and broaden the work of the AMA, not only for the sake of Maritain's message but also for the lonely academics, like myself, hungry for a community to support their work.

I was intrigued by Maritain's notion of aesthetics, a conception that did not begin with theories of form or interpretation but with the artistic habits of artists themselves. It's not that Maritain considered the contemplation of aesthetic form unimportant, but that he thought it was putting the cart before the horse, so to speak. Since artworks arise from the creative intuition of artists, a philosophical understanding of "art" must focus on the habit of making works of fine art, the virtue called art, and artworks themselves.

Maritain's inspiration for this kind of aesthetics went back to Aristotle and Plato through their medieval interpreters, particularly Aquinas. In addition, Maritain's circle of friendship included a who's who of prominent artists — Georges Rouault, Jean Cocteau, Maurice Sachs, Léon Bloy, Arthur Lourié, Erik Satie, Julian Green, Georges Bernanos, André Gide, Igor Stravinsky. His ability to befriend artists continued after he moved to America in the 1940s as is typified by his relationship with and influence on Allen Tate, Caroline Gordon, Robert Lowell, Robert Fitzgerald, and John Howard Griffin, among others.

By focusing on art as the habit of making Maritain was able to address several of the central concerns that arise when religion and art come into contact. The most important of these are questions of artistic freedom, namely, these two: how prominent a role should religious symbols play in the artwork? and, should artworks always have an uplifting moral influence?

Maritain surprised people with his answer, and still does. He defended the freedom of the artist from the

Jacques Maritain – "The habit of the fine artist, he argued, is ordered to the making of beautiful things; as such its goal is beauty, not truth."

overt use of religious references and from the demand of moralists to avoid the depictions of sin. The habit of the fine artist, he argued, is ordered to the making of beautiful things; as such its goal is beauty, not truth. To judge the quality of an artwork by the criterion used to judge, say, a theological essay, is to mistake what an artwork is *for*. Similarly, the moralist who judges a work by its morally offensive contents, or lack of them, is missing the point as well. It's no wonder Maritain shared such a deep friendship with the novelist Julian Green, who explored all the inner recesses of the sinful heart.

Being familiar with the history of art, Maritain was able to illustrate from secular and religious art how the preponderance of theoretical concerns by an artist usually ended up ruining, or at least weakening, his art. This line of argument became the core of his 1952 Mellon Lectures at the National Gallery in Washington, D.C., published as *Creative Intuition in Art and Poetry*, a work which at once celebrated the spiritual significance of modern art while showing that surrealism was an example of art turning away from beauty in favor of inspired preaching.

For me, Maritain's aesthetics came at just the right time. I was beginning my teaching career at Mercer University in Atlanta, and I was eager to treat literature, music, and visual arts in my classroom. His distinction, drawing upon Aristotle, between the habits of art and prudence allowed me to make an argument to my Southern Baptist students about why they were being asked to read novels such as

Flaubert's *Madame Bovary* and Walker Percy's *Love in the Ruins* in my classroom.

Also my encounter with Jacques Maritain the man came at just the right time. As a young man he had been a student of biology and philosophy at the Sorbonne. His religious sensibilities were nil; he had been raised in a nonpracticing family of liberal Protestants with socialist sympathies. But his penchant for philosophy got the better of him, and he began to discuss his doubts with a young Russian émigré also at the Sorbonne, Raïssa Oumansov. They each had deep anxiety, as only college students can, over the existence of an absolute upon which to base their beliefs. One day walking through the Jardin des Plantes in Paris they vowed that if within one year they had not discovered some absolute basis for life they would commit suicide together. They were saved from that fate by the lectures of Henri Bergson, who showed them a way to affirm an absolute in a world of time and fluctuating appearances. A short time later they would meet the spiritual writer Léon Bloy and his family whose piety and extreme, apparently chosen, poverty led them both into the Church.

What most admirers of Maritain don't remember is that Maritain started his writing career by breaking publicly with Bergson over the nature of human intelligence and particularly the ability of intellectual concepts to capture reality. Indeed, all of Maritain's early work, including his aesthetics, constitutes a retrieval of human intelligence, an affirmation of the intellect's ability to know extramental reality through its immaterial action. Thus, when he noted the dangerous emphasis on phenomenology after the Vatican Council, his reaction was not inconsistent.

All the major works of Maritain's first decade as an author take a combative pose against opponents of Thomistic realism: from his 1914 critique of Bergson's intuitionism, to *Art and Scholasticism* in 1920, which takes aim at the Renaissance selfhood and the decadence of so-called "religious art," followed by *Theonas* (1921), his *General Introduction to Philosophy* (1922), *Antimoderne* (1922), *St. Thomas Aquinas, Apostle of Modern Times* (1923), and *Reflections on Intelligence* (1924), all culminating in the still controversial *Three Reformers* of 1925.

Although Maritain's rhetoric became less abrasive with age, many of his later works contain strongly worded polemics, namely, his lectures on the philosophy of history and on the philosophy of education (*Education at the Crossroads*, 1943), with their attacks on Hegel and Dewey, his treatment of immanentism and fideism in *Integral Humanism,* his books on anti-Semitism and the Nazi and the Communist threats, his response to Sartre, Nietzsche, and Kierkegaard in *Existence and the Existent,* and the chapter on Kant in the lectures given in 1951 during his last year of active teaching and published as *Moral Philosophy.*

No, the harsh words Maritain spoke toward his opponents were not at issue — Maritain never shrank from a fight. The issue, rather, was that these opponents were in fashion. Whereas Maritain as democrat, as liberal, as humanist was acceptable, Maritain as Thomist was not. This attitude still persists in most Catholic institutions to the present day. Maritain's plight represents in miniature the tumult in Catholic intellectual life over the past forty years. At some future date, Maritain, and the legacy he represented, will be vindicated. But at present many Catholic intellectuals and pundits seek, in vain, to marry Catholicism with postmodernism. Maritain's criticism struck too close to the bone for those Catholics involved in culture and politics. He had helped people to break loose, to claim their intellectual and political freedom, and now, it seemed, he was admonishing them to give it up. This symbol to the world's Catholic intellectuals, so designated by Paul VI at the end of the Vatican Council, was sounding as if he wanted to bring back the bygone days. But the truth is that Maritain in the *Peasant* points his finger at our consumption of intellectual fashion "with all the glamour and happy arrogance of a reason maddened by frenzy for novelty."

Indeed what still seems to me one of the most powerful and prophetic aspects of *Peasant* is its depiction of "logophobia." How much more we have learned about the hatred of reason in the postmodern world of deconstruction and gender/race epistemologies since the heyday of mere existentialism. The question of restoring the ordinate relation of intelligence to being was always Maritain's major concern as a philosopher. Maritain defended the sense of objectivity at the heart of the Catholic tradition

Maritain sought to explain and to defend a logocentric world where being is fundamentally intelligible. The same concern with restoring the intellect motivates his last critique of idealism or the ideosophy, as he calls it in the *Peasant*. Ideosophers, according to Maritain, are not philosophers because by grasping first at mind they miss the true *starting point* for knowledge, which is the encounter of the mind with the reality external to it.

Other of Maritain's mocking phrases such as "epistemological time-worship" or "chronolatry" seem perfectly suited to the influences he was seeking to counteract in the wake of Vatican II. He predicted correctly the phrase "Vatican II" would be used to justify any and all demands for structural change in the Catholic Church. Those tempted to say he lacked "historical-mindedness" should notice that Maritain starts from a historical analysis of modern Manicheanism in seeking to understand the mania in the 1960s for "up-to-dateness." For 150 years a pervasive Christian pessimism toward the world, he argued, not only subverted the Church's understanding of its temporal mission but also suppressed its appreciation of secular progress. What we are witnessing in the present age, he said, is the compensation for that suppression. "Why be astonished that at the very announcement of a Council . . . the enormous unconscious weight . . . burst open in a kind of explosion that does no honor to human intelligence?"

To his friends and admirers it is clear that *The Peasant of the Garonne*, published in 1966 (Eng. trans. 1968), cost Maritain a great deal — if not his earthly happiness then without doubt much of his reputation.

In the United States anticipation of Maritain's book was so intense that translated excerpts of the *Peasant* were being circulated before the complete translation was available in early 1968. Prior to its publication, Thomas Merton predicted that the book would be dismissed without being read because of the negative hearsay from abroad. In fact, Merton proved to be at least partially right. The stateside critics for the most part panned the *Peasant.* Robert Graham, representing the consensual view, wrote in *America* that Maritain was being "cast . . . as a Brutus who stabbed aggiornamento in the back." *The Peasant of the Garonne,* he agreed, had repudiated what its author had spent his whole life defending and concluded that "Maritain is now afraid the fire he helped to kindle is getting out of control."

In France, where the controversy erupted, *Peasant* was the best-selling book of nonfiction in January 1967. Within four months of its publication seventy thousand copies had been sold in seven printings. Following the subsequent attacks, Maritain stood accused by both sides of turning against his friends, of "treason," "disloyalty," "injustice," and of just having lived too long.

Having returned to Europe from the United States in 1961 following the death of his wife, Raïssa, Jacques Maritain — an acclaimed champion of democratic liberalism, international cooperation, human rights, social reform, an increased role for laity in the Church, and progressive movements in art and culture — died in 1973 branded a "reactionary."

In my view Maritain lived long enough to see that his readers, like all readers, pick and choose. He saw that many of those who embraced his political views, particularly his pioneering work on human rights, didn't understand that without the Thomistic anthropology and epistemology the whole project of grounding human rights in human nature came tumbling down. Without an immaterial soul, human beings don't deserve any greater respect than a horse or a cow, and without an immaterial intellect that grasps universal truths we cannot claim to know any more than a horse or cow about what is right or wrong.

Anyone who wants to find a way out of the present postmodern maze needs only to consult the early Maritain, who broke free from Bergson, and the later

Maritain, who schematized the "Degrees of Knowledge." Thus Maritain gave me the grounds for a wholehearted affirmation of Christian intelligence and Christian art, while at the same time knowing when they need to be kept from intruding on each other.

✟ Twenty-One ✟

QUICK-EY'D
LOVE

THE COMPOSER Ralph Vaughn Williams introduced me to a poem on love by George Herbert
in his musical setting of "Five Mystical Songs." This
song cycle remains among the most powerful mar-
riages of word and music that I know of. And the
Herbert poem beginning "Love bade me welcome
but my soul drew back" contains for me just about
everything that needs to be said about love.

I'm just one of many who have been moved by
this poem, one of three that Herbert dedicated to
the theme of love. The Jewish-born philosopher and
mystic Simone Weil said that she felt Christ's presence while reciting Herbert's poem: "Christ himself
came down and took me." She recited this poem so
often that it became to her a prayer.

174

For me the poem sets out the basic problem of love in dramatic terms, the struggle between the self and others, whether our neighbors or God.

> Love bade me welcome, yet my soul drew back,
>   Guilty of dust and sin.
> But quick-ey'd Love, observing me grow slack
>   From my first entrance in,
> Drew nearer to me, sweetly questioning
>   If I lack'd anything.
> "A guest," I answer'd, "worthy to be here";
>   Love said, "You shall be he."
> "I, the unkind, the ungrateful? ah my dear,
>   I cannot look on thee."

As a teenager I was drawn to the communion of Southern Baptists by their strong sense of fellowship, their congregational singing, the impassioned personal prayers, and their forthright confession of moral failure and repentance. All this seemed an answer to my sense of being mired in selfishness, which was in various ways reinforced by the common unhappiness of my ordinary middle-class upbringing. I sought a way out of the preoccupation with my self, and the exuberant generosity of the local Baptist church offered that.

But there was a drawback. Among my Baptist friends one kind of unworthiness was addressed, but another was put in its place. The basic moral un-worthiness, "guilty of dust and sin," was replaced by a kind of metaphysical unworthiness. Evangelicals view human nature as fallen and the work of grace as extrinsic to an unredeemable human nature. In other words, I was asked to live in a radically divided world, described best in Luther's words, "at once justified, at once a sinner" (*simul justus, simul peccator*).

This hard distinction leads, I believe, to the evan-gelical mistrust of human works of all kinds, not just claims to good works, but to the works of culture — the arts, philosophy, the humanities. Philosophy was studied among Baptists primarily to find out what it was lacking, how it was in basic discord with Scrip-tures. There was no spirit of cooperation, no instinct to wed the truth of philosophy with revealed truth.

Love itself becomes problematic in this universe where all things human are viewed under the species of fallenness. The implications are clearly shown by Lutheran theologian Anders Nygren in his now-classic work *Agape and Eros*. Nygren's basic point is that in the Catholic tradition represented by Aquinas

human love or eros is considered capable of uniting with grace or agape to produce morally worthy
acts. Eros is always acquisitive in its desire to fulfill a need and seek satisfaction. Nygren offers an
able critique of this synthesis of agape and eros from
a Lutheran position, making sure that human beings get no credit for any cooperation with God's
overwhelming grace.

> Love took my hand and smiling did reply,
> > "Who made the eyes but I?"
> "Truth, Lord, but I have marr'd them; let my shame
> > Go where it doth deserve."
> "And know you not," says Love, "who bore the blame?"
> > "My dear, then I will serve."
> "You must sit down," says Love, "and taste my meat."
> > So I did sit and eat.

Herbert's narrator, Love herself, has no such worries about human nature: "Who made the eyes but
I?" God as creator is a source of goodness in our nature that cannot be destroyed. Yes, this goodness has
been "marr'd" by sin, but that stain has been removed
by the Christ, "who bore the blame."

The eucharistic image of the final lines, "taste
my meat," completes the journey from estrangement

to communion. This is not the grace laid over the penitent's shoulder like a cloak (Martin Luther's metaphor) but a grace that penetrates the very body of the believer: "So I did sit and eat."

Aquinas writes over and over that "grace perfects nature; it does not destroy it." Agape does not obliterate eros; grace strengthens human love, inwardly ordering it once again to God. Thus my struggle with love only began with the burden of selfishness; the problem of what to do with oneself never comes to an end, in this life. But how can self-love be legitimate when the self is made for others and God? That was the question remaining for me. I knew that learning to love did not require leaving the self entirely behind, but I lacked a conceptual grasp of how the self becomes included in the dynamics of agape.

Some may chuckle at the fact that I was reading about the idea of love, trying to get a handle on love as a concept. But since love is the most difficult thing we are called to do, what is more natural than trying to understand it?

Two classic works on love freed me from long-standing existential puzzles: why do friends come and go, and why does marriage lose its passion?

Thomas Aquinas – "Aquinas writes over and over that 'grace perfects nature, it does not destroy it.' Agape does not obliterate eros; grace strengthens human love, inwardly ordering it once again to God."

The section in Aristotle's *Ethics* (1155a–1172a16)
devoted to the three forms of friendship makes a
simple distinction between the types of friendship
founded on pleasure or usefulness and those based
upon a mutual vision of life. It's much more likely
that the reasons for two people finding each other
useful or pleasurable are going to change than the
vision uniting them. Therefore friends will come and
go when these conditions change.

Frankly I was greatly relieved to read this because
I long harbored a sense of insecurity about the loss
of some friendships. When I took account of my
longtime friends, I realized that Aristotle was exactly
right: they were the ones who saw the world much
the same way I did, and their bond with me never
changed.

Those who are married commonly joke, and sometimes complain, about the passing of erotic passion in
their relationship. The intense feelings of courtship,
marriage, and the honeymoon are eventually replaced by the ordinariness of work, children, and
paying the mortgage. Somewhere along the way, perhaps it was because of my romantic temperament, I
expected the passion would never subside. I experienced, the hard way, that passion does subside, and

I was foolish not to realize that the love that follows is better.

Perhaps I was imbued with what Denis de Rougement terms the "myth of romantic love." In his *Love in the Western World,* de Rougement traces this myth to the troubadour poets of the twelfth century in southern France. These were the traveling poet-singers who entertained at the feudal courts of kings and queens like Eleanor of Aquitaine. The essence of their message was that love's passion thrives on having an obstacle to overcome, for example, a single man loving a married woman, particularly a woman from a higher class, such as Tristan's love for his queen Isolde. The best-known case is that of Romeo and Juliet, two lovers trying to overcome the opposition of quarreling families.

De Rougement offered insight into the way I resisted the commonplace demands of love. I also saw the way I tried to create an artificial intensity in my relationships. No doubt this led to unfortunate and destructive behavior on my part. "Truth, Lord, but I have marr'd them; let my shame / Go where it doth deserve." I am blessed that I have not gotten what I deserved.

Thomas Merton records in his memoir *The Seven Storey Mountain* how his discovery of Etienne Gilson's *The Spirit of Mediaeval Philosophy* in the stacks of the Columbia University Library helped lead him to the Church. It was my reading of Gilson that enabled me to conceptualize the relation of love of the self to God. In short, what you give away comes back to you, but the self you give up comes back in a different aspect. As Gilson puts it, relying on the mystical theology of St. Bernard, "To say that if man of necessity loves himself he cannot love God with disinterested love, is to forget that to love God with disinterested love is man's true way of loving himself" (*The Spirit of Mediaeval Philosophy*). In other words, loving God is rewarded but without being consciously sought, and this quality of spiritual disinterest is the challenge of the spiritual life. Gilson, pressing further, puts it this way, "To love God is, in a way, to make God love Himself in us, as He Loves Himself in Himself." It's no historical accident that Bernard was writing at the same time that the troubador poets were entertaining the ladies at court.

The final stop in the road of understanding love, not doing it, was, of course, the mother of God.

Mary is the fullest representation of the human intersection of divine and human love. Mary is the mediatrix of all graces; her very body was used for the redemption of the world. It's not surprising that the greatest of all twentieth-century Protestant theologians, Karl Barth, would argue that Mariology represents the essence of Catholicism — the human cooperation in redemption — and, as such, must be rejected. Barth is absolutely right that Mary represents the heart of the Church: what the Church is invisibly and should be visibly is present in Mary. She represents the maternity of the Church both literally and figuratively: Mary gave birth to Jesus Christ and represents the necessity of nature receiving grace, leading to the generation of new life, our own and others.

About a year before my conversion I was jolted by the sudden departure of someone I loved but whose love I had not treated well. The hurt was compounded by my sense of failure. I spent many months in a daze hoping to win her back but without any progress. I was to blame and I knew it.

Out of desperation I went to my local parish, Immaculate Heart of Mary, the one where I would eventually receive my first communion. On the wall to the left of the altar was a portrait of Mary. The picture was nothing great artistically but the face and eyes of Mary were arresting in their loveliness. I spent hours over the next few weeks praying before that picture. As I prayed I realized I was praying to a person who knew all about love and its suffering.

My prayers brought me both relief from my loss and a sense of forgiveness for my failure. I saw in her example that love required the complete "gift of self." I had been too preoccupied with myself, my work, and making my way in the world to make that gift. My love had restricted itself to providing for my own needs and little more. I, too, was called to cooperate in salvation by growing in love.

My conversion a year later did not miraculously cure my problem with self-absorption. I am still converting, no longer from evangelicalism, but from the stubborn self-regard that we all share in our fallen human nature. Conversion never ends, even for those who have always felt at home in the Church.

I leave it to others, my friends and family, to evaluate my progress. What I know is that I have been given every possible opportunity to enter the Body of Christ. As in the Herbert poem, Love has never abandoned me, never accepted my excuses, or let me run away. At each turn, I have heard her say, "You must sit down … and taste my meat."

Between that verse and the next, "so I did sit and eat," there is a mysterious silence, a missing link in the argument of the poem. Why did he sit and eat? Why did I? The silence exists because at the moment of turning toward God all explanations fail. God fills in the silence.

The lure of God's beauty, of his works, of those made by human hands, may stir the heart to seek him but fails to explain how he is found, or we are found by him.

Converts such as I can point to signs and wonders along the way of their journey with gratitude and with hope that others will be similarly moved. But their stories themselves testify to the multitude of ways that God makes himself present to our eyes and ears. What remains universal, however, is that God came down, that He comes down every day and beckons us in him to rest.

PHOTO CREDITS

Mortimer Adler: Deal W. Hudson, personal photo.

St. Augustine: El Greco.

Louis Bouyer: Ignatius Press.

Frederick Delius: Lionel Carley, *Delius A Life in Letters,
1909–1934,* Scolar Press in association with The Delius Trust.

Julian Green: Marion Boyars Publishers.

James Hitchcock: Dr. Hitchcock's personal photo.

Erasmo Leiva-Merikakis: Ignatius Press.

Father Richard Lopez: *Georgia Bulletin* photo by Linda Schaefer

William Lynch: From the cover of Father Lynch's book
The Integrating Mind (Sheed and Ward, 1962).

Jacques Maritain: University Archives, Hesburgh Library at
the University of Notre Dame.

Flannery O'Connor: Flannery O'Connor Collection, Ina
Dillard Russell Library, Georgia College and State University.

Walker Percy: Father Patrick H. Samway, S.J., Patrick H.
Samway Collection, Monroe Library, Loyola University, New
Orleans.

Thomas Aquinas: Museo de S. Marco, Beato Angelico.

Sigrid Undset: Kevin Chadwick

INDEX
OF NAMES

Adam, 121
Adler, Caroline, 112
Adler, Mortimer J., 112–14, 117, 120
Aquinas, Thomas, 43, 57, 68, 73, 74, 78–79, 90, 94, 95, 103, 107–10, 112, 126–28, 131, 138, 145, 160, 162, 163, 176, 178
Aristotle, 14, 39, 40, 56, 66–68, 74, 77, 107, 163, 180
Augustine, St., 26–29, 43, 66, 94, 132–33, 136, 158

Bach, Johann Sebastian, 132
Balthasar, Hans Urs von, 53, 54, 94, 122, 123, 125, 131
Barth, Karl, 136, 183
Baudelaire, Charles-Pierre, 54, 57, 61–64
Beatles, 40
Beecham, Sir Thomas, 21
Bergson, Henri, 166, 167, 172
Bernanos, Georges, 54, 142, 163
Bernard, St., 182

Bloy, Léon, 163, 166
Bouyer, Louis, 54, 80–84
Brando, Marlon, 26

Callahan, Morley, 143
Calvin, John, 82, 136
Chateaubriand, François, 61
Chesterton, G. K., 98, 136
Cocteau, Jean, 163
Coleridge, Samuel Taylor, 61
Congar, Yves, 54
Curran, Charles, 93, 94

Daniélou, Jean, 54
Dante Alighieri, 54, 139, 141, 145, 159
Darwin, Charles, 34
Day, Dorothy, 139
Debussy, Claude, 40
Delius, Frederick, 21–22
Descartes, René, 14, 114, 117, 118, 120
Dewey, John, 168
Dostoevsky, Fyodor, 130, 133
Duval, Jeanne, 62

187

Index of Names

Einstein, Albert, 34
Eleanor of Aquitaine, 181
Ellis, Alice Thomas, 143
Escrivá, St. Josémaría, 134
Evans, Arthur, 56
Eve, 121

Fessio, Joseph, 80, 83, 84
Fitzgerald, Robert, 163
Flaubert, Gustave, 166
Francis, St., 33, 136
Frank, Anne, 42
Freud, Sigmund, 34, 65
Froelich, Karlfried, 26,

Garrigou-Lagrange, Reginald, 136
Gide, André, 163
Gilby, Thomas, O.P., 77
Gilson, Etienne, 134, 182
Gordon, Caroline, 163
Graham, Billy, 24
Graham, Robert, 171
Green, Ann, 153
Green, Graham, 54
Green, Julian, 54, 138, 152–60, 163, 165
Green, Mary Hartridge, 152
Griffin, John Howard, 163

Hansen, Ron, 143
Hardon, John, 108, 109
Hassler, Jon, 143
Heer, Frederich, 150
Hegel, G. W. F., 168
Hemingway, Ernest, 143
Hendricks, Jean, 58, 60, 61, 80
Herbert, George, 174, 177, 184

Herod, 18
Hesla, David, 56
Hitchcock, James, 92, 95–98, 102
Hume, David, 14

James, William 112
John, Elton, 40
John XXIII, Pope, 99
John Paul II, Pope, 89, 97, 99
Joyce, James, 51

Kant, Immanuel, 14, 168
Kierkegaard, Søren, 52, 57, 61–65, 77, 141, 146, 168

Lassus, Roland de, 101
Leiva-Merikakis, Erasmo, 53–54, 80, 84, 85, 90, 91, 92, 103–4, 108
Lindgren, Torgny, 143
Lopez, Richard, 104–9
Lourie, Arthur, 163
Lowell, Robert, 163
Lubac, Henri de, 54, 94, 97–98
Luther, Martin, 82, 136, 176, 178
Lynch, William F., 46–52, 65, 102, 122, 123

Mancini, Matt, 107, 108
Mancini, Missy, 108
Maritain, Jacques, 43, 68, 72, 92, 94, 95, 107, 116, 120, 122, 123, 131, 145, 161–73
Maritain, Raïssa Oumansov, 166, 172
Marty, Martin, 32

Index of Names

Mary, 47, 54, 64, 65, 106, 183, 184
Mauriac, François, 153
McCord, James, 15
McDowell, Malcolm, 26
McInerny, Ralph, 93, 143
Merton, Thomas, 134, 171, 182
Milton, John, 41

Niebuhr, H. Richard, 136
Niebuhr, Reinhold, 136
Nietzsche, Friedrich Wilhelm, 21, 22, 39, 40, 57, 61–64, 168
Novak, Michael, 93
Novalis, 61
Nygren, Anders, 176, 177

Occam, William of, 150
O'Connor, Edwin, 143
O'Connor, Flannery, 54, 57, 108, 141–42
Olsen, Regina, 62

Paul VI, Pope, 93, 169
Paul, St., 78
Percy, Walker, 117–20, 141, 166
Plato, 12, 14, 27, 42, 43, 66, 113, 126, 128, 132, 163
Powers, J. F., 143
Pythagoras, 33

Ravel, Maurice J., 40
Read, Piers Paul, 143

Rilke, Rainer Maria, 54
Rouault, Georges, 163
Rougement, Denis de, 181
Russell, Ken, 21

Sabatier, Madame, 63
Sachs, Maurice, 163
Saliers, Don, 57
Salome, 63
Sartre, Jean-Paul, 168
Satie, Erik, 163
Sayers, Dorothy, 126
Simon, Tony and Judy, 162
Socrates, 42, 132
Sophocles, 46, 47, 52
Spark, Muriel, 143
Steiner, George, 70
Stravinsky, Igor, 163

Tate, Allen, 163
Teilhard de Chardin, Pierre, 161
Tillich, Paul, 136

Undset, Sigrid, 139–41

Vianney, Jean-Marie, 142
Victoria, Tomás Luis de, 101

Ward, Maisie, 136
Waugh, Evelyn, 54, 137
Weil, Simone, 174
Whitman, Walt, 21
Williams, Ralph Vaughn, 174
Wordsworth, William, 61

OF RELATED INTEREST
BY MARK S. MASSA, S.J.

CATHOLICS AND AMERICAN CULTURE
*Fulton Sheen, Dorothy Day, and the Notre Dame
Football Team*

While in the early years of the twentieth century Catholics in America were for the most part distrusted outsiders with respect to the dominant culture, by the 1960s the mainstream of American Catholicism was in many ways "the culture's loudest and most uncritical cheerleader." Mark Massa explores the rich irony in this postwar transition, beginning with the heresy case of Leonard Feeney, examining key figures such as Fulton Sheen, Thomas Merton, and John F. Kennedy, and concluding with a look at the University of Notre Dame and the transformed status of American Catholic higher education.

0-8245-1955-8, $19.95 paperback

ANTI-CATHOLICISM IN AMERICA
The Last Acceptable Prejudice

One of the most important books in religion this year is a tour-de-force of new investigation, scholarly rigor, storytelling, and humor. In this authoritative work, Mark Massa, program director of Fordham University's Center for American Catholic Studies, reveals how American Catholics' distinctive way of viewing the world is constantly misunderstood — and attacked — by outsiders.

0-8245-2129-3, $24.95 hardcover

crossroad

ALSO OF INTEREST

Lorenzo Albacete
GOD AT THE RITZ
Attraction to Infinity

"Lorenzo Albacete is one of a kind, and so is *God at the Ritz*. The book, like the monsignor, crackles with humor, warmth, and intellectual excitement. Reading it is like having a stay-up-all-night, jump-out-of-your-chair, have-another-double-espresso marathon conversation with one of the world's most swashbuckling talkers. Conversation, heck — this is a papal bull session!"

— Hendrik Herzberg, *The New Yorker Magazine*

0-8245-1951-5, $19.95 hardcover

Also available in Spanish:
Dios en el Ritz
0-8245-2113-7, $19.95 paperback

Please support your local bookstore,
or call 1-800-707-0670 for Customer Service.

For a free catalog, write us at

THE CROSSROAD PUBLISHING COMPANY
481 Eighth Avenue, Suite 1550
New York, NY 10001

Visit our website at
www.crossroadpublishing.com
All prices subject to change.

crossroad